DALIT FREEDOM *and* BEYOND

THE STORY OF THE GOOD SHEPHERD CHURCH MOVEMENT

Dalit Freedom — And Beyond
by Joseph D'souza

Copyright © 2004 by Joseph D'souza
Abridged edition 2012
Revised edition 2015

ISBN 978-0-9764290-3-6

Published by
Good Shepherd-Dayspring Ministries
P.O. Box 3309
Virginia Beach, VA 23454

"Joseph D'souza has taken a prominent role in supporting Dalits, who have suffered religiously-based discrimination from the country's high-caste Hindus for millennia."

Stan Guthrie
Christianity Today

"Dalit Freedom and Beyond is an extraordinary journey of reformation. The story of the Good Shepherd Church movement is remarkable! It's like witnessing the Book of Acts and the early church. I am both humbled and proud to be Dr. D'souza's friend and partner in this historic transformational church growth movement. Every Christian should read this story and ask how to become engaged."

John Gilman
Founder, Dayspring International

"The Good Shepherd Church movement has done extraordinary work introducing our Lord Jesus to millions of history's most disenfranchised peoples. I heartily endorse this ministry and rejoice in the impact that the Good Shepherd Church is having across the Indian subcontinent."

Jack Hayford
Founder and Chancellor Kings University

"I don't have words to express how important I think this book is. I believe it is one of the greatest challenges facing the Church around the world at this time. Please get extra copies to give to friends and PLEASE get involved in the Dalit Freedom Movement. Let's also mobilize prayer for this situation."

George Verwer, Founder, OM International
and Chief Patron Good Shepherd/OM India Ministries

"I will be eternally grateful that someone placed a copy of Dr. Joseph D'souza's heroic saga of The Dalit Freedom Movement in my hands. It galvanized me personally as one who has long fought for the rights and dignity of oppressed people. It transformed my congregation from a sleepy church into a world changing force. Run to the bookstore. Beg, borrow, or do whatever you have to in order to get a copy of this book. Devour every page, and then let the Holy Spirit use it to expand your vision, inspire your faith, and transform your world."

Dr. Robert Petterson
Senior Pastor, Covenant Church of Naples

"In the context of a post-Durban UN conference against caste and racial discrimination, the work done by Dr. D'souza and the committed team that works within organizations like the aicc, the Dalit Freedom Movement and various other groups, has brought about a sea of change in the understanding of Western societies, states, media, and more particularly the Church.

"This small manifesto that Dr. D'souza has written helps the world understand his position on the question of religious freedom for Dalits, Tribals and OBCs, and also the role of the Church. It brings out the history of struggles endured by the oppressed masses of India and works out a program for liberation of the untouchable and oppressed communities in India. In the future, the campaigns of global human rights leaders, whether religious or secular, should focus on the abolition of untouchability and caste discrimination in India."

Dr. Kancha Ilaiah, Professor, Osmania University
Author, Why I am Not a Hindu

"[Joseph D'souza] is a leading figure in the life of the evangelical church in India, a key leader in one of the most effective ministries in that great land [Good Shepherd-Dayspring Ministries] ... and **undoubtedly one of the most godly and knowledgeable people about the work of the gospel in what will shortly be the most populous nation in the world.** He speaks powerfully ... and I warmly commend him to the Church worldwide. We all need to hear about India and no one can speak to us more clearly than Joseph D'souza."

Stuart Briscoe
Minister at Large, Elmbrook Church, Wisconsin

"The movement is nothing short of miraculous. It has changed thousands of people over the last decade, including me. And when a leader is changed, a church, a community, a nation has the chance to experience something beyond imagination ... and as you read you will be changed! Our prayer is that you, too, will be moved and join us as we fight for freedom."

Matthew Cork
Lead Pastor, Friends Church
Yorba Linda, California

DALIT
FREEDOM
and BEYOND
THE STORY OF THE
GOOD SHEPHERD CHURCH MOVEMENT

THE EPIC

STRUGGLE

TO END

DALIT

SLAVERY

JOSEPH D'SOUZA

CONTENTS

FOREWORD:

A NEW GUIDE FOR NEW ACTION

Joseph D'souza is one of the world's great Christian leaders, fully sensitized to the Dalit plight in ideology, practice, and family, even though he comes from the upper caste sections of Indian Christians in Mangalore. He carries the great traditions of white Christians who raised the banner of revolt against slavery and racism in their nations. He is the President of the All India Christian Council (aicc) and its international counterpart in the USA, Canada, Brasil, the UK and elsewhere, the Dalit Freedom Network. He is one of the first major Christian leaders to globalize the issue of caste and to work for the abolition of caste and untouchability.

The aicc was born during a crisis of persecution and with the confidence of major and minor Christian denominations and churches in India. After coming to power in the Indian Government in 1996, the Hindutva organizations launched an attack on the Indian Church and all its denominations. The aicc was formed as an umbrella organization to protect the right of all Christian churches to propagate their religion and to ensure their human rights. In 2001, the aicc declared its support for the Dalit-Bahujan liberation struggles. The Hindutva organizations and the Bharatiya Janata Party (BJP) were historically strongly against spiritual equality for the Dalits, Tribals and Other Backward Castes (OBCs).

The priestly caste, the Brahmins, was against the lower castes gaining spiritual equality. Brahmins alone hold the most powerful position, temple priests, in their hands. They are also opposed to communicating with Hindu gods in any language other than Sanskrit. Historically, this language was not supposed to be learned by the Dalits, Tribals and OBCs. Because of this spiritual oppression, already four major regions of ancient India have gone into the fold of Islam: Afghanistan, Pakistan, Bangladesh and Kashmir. The violent clashes between Hinduism and Islam in the Indian sub-continent created conditions of conflict, including all forms of terrorism. Dr. D'souza realizes that abolishing caste in India could solve the problem of Indian terrorism.

Christian missionaries introduced the concept of a universal education and also English as a language that can be used in the Church, State and civil society. Since the dominant Christian churches were also in the hands of upper caste converts, they did not think of giving spiritual equality and an English education to the lower castes. The Hindutva leaders educated their children in English, but abused and attacked the Church when it started serving the Dalits, Tribals and OBCs. The aicc, under the leadership of Dr. D'souza, took a categorical stand in opposing caste practices within the Church, as well as in Hindu society. It challenged the Hindutva forces on all fronts. It openly declared that the right to choose one's religion is a universal human right. The Christian Church should openly welcome the Dalits, Tribals, OBCs and others if they choose to embrace Christianity. The world knows well that religion is not bound by territorial national boundaries. The people's nationalist right is to choose any faith they prefer. Hindu Brahmanism stagnated Indian society by forcefully keeping people inside caste culture. Only spiritual democracy can move this stagnant society toward change. Without establishing spiritual democracy, even India's political democracy may evaporate in the near future.

Necessary professions like shepherding, tilling the soil to produce food, buffalo-, bull- and cow-rearing, tanning and making goods out of animal skin, making pots out of soft soils, and climbing trees to cut fruit to harness natural drinks were declared tasks of spiritual pollution in India. In a word, the dignity of labor was destroyed. By taking a clear stand on caste and the right to religion, Dr. D'souza has shown a new path for the world and for India.

He says repeatedly that the battle for Dalit-Bahujan rights

to equality should be fought on all fronts, especially globally and particularly in America and Europe. The understanding of the Western world about caste and untouchability must change. India has been presented to them through the eyes of Brahmanism's interpretation of the Indian reality. There is a deliberate silence on the issue of caste discrimination and atrocities in India. The magnitude of the atrocities continues to baffle Indian society. As a result, Dr. D'souza initiated a worldwide campaign against caste and untouchability. His efforts have started to change the mindset of the Western Church.

In the context of a post-Durban UN conference against caste and racial discrimination, the work done by Dr. D'souza and the committed team that works within organizations like the aicc, the Dalit Freedom Movement and various other groups, has brought about a sea of change in the understanding of Western societies, states, media, and more particularly the Church. This small manifesto helps the world understand Dr. D'souza's position on the question of religious freedom for Dalits, Tribals and OBCs, and also the role of the Church. It brings out the history of struggles endured by the oppressed masses of India and works out a program for liberation of the untouchable and oppressed communities in India. In the future, the campaigns of global human rights leaders, whether religious or secular, should focus on the abolition of untouchability and caste discrimination in India.

The world movement for socio-spiritual, political and economic equality becomes meaningless if caste and untouchability remain as they are in India. Dr. D'souza's efforts and clarion call for spiritual liberation of the Dalit-Bahujans of India gives a new hope for the oppressed and exploited masses of India and around the world.

Dr. Kancha Ilaiah
Professor of Political Science, Osmania University
Author of Why I am Not a Hindu
October 17, 2004
Hyderabad, India

PRELUDE TO
DALIT FREEDOM AND BEYOND

THE GOOD SHEPHERD CHURCH

The location of the exciting story of the Good Shepherd Church Movement is in the 2,000-year-old Indian Church. With congregations across India, we are indeed an inter-caste, inter-racial and inter-ethnic Church. We believe in the transforming power of the gospel in all areas of life.

When Jesus called the Apostle Thomas to India it was to follow Jesus' mandate of Kingdom mission as found in Luke 4:18-20 which indicates that "since Thomas' time the people of India have found hope in Jesus and his message of the Kingdom of God."

In post-Independent India, this message of the life of Christ has resonated with India's masses. The colonial trappings of the gospel have disappeared. Jesus is not the God and Savior of the white ruling classes. He is the God of the poor, the downtrodden, the oppressed, the sick and needy as described in Luke 4.

**The Good Shepherd Church is fanatic
about its commitment to Jesus' mandate.**

It is clear to us that we can make a significant contribution to India's greatness as we bring Jesus' transformation to millions. Some accuse us of 'breaking' India when all that we have done is make India great. We believe Jesus is for a strong, united India where diverse cultures and peoples live side by side and build a great nation.

All that we continue to do is to reach out to people with Jesus' light and love to those who want freedom from exploitation, ignorance, illiteracy and slavery.

The Constitution of India allows us the freedom to practice and propagate the faith of our choice. For Christians this is about following and keeping the commands of Jesus. The great commandment for us is to love God and love our neighbor regardless of their religious affiliations.

As we have engaged with the poor, the downtrodden, the oppressed and with women, we work out the Kingdom of God on earth.

Decades ago we had stated that the Dalits and the oppressed masses would know our unconditional love regardless of whether they turn to Christ or not. We stand by our commitment. Christ does not teach us to love only those who will follow him.

The Good Shepherd Church movement does not believe that Jesus has asked us to conquer the world or rule the world or rule a nation.

Jesus' Kingdom is different from the political kingdoms of this world.

Jesus' Kingdom is about the power of God at work in the hearts of people and communities.

It is about a deep, personal and societal moral and ethical change. It is about obedience to God and the loving of our neighbor just as we love ourselves. The world and India would be a better place if Christians followed Jesus' commands.

Jesus' Kingdom is also not about becoming the majority in a nation or in the world. Jesus was clear that even though every human being has the offer of his free love and salvation, it is the minority who will follow him. This was true during Jesus' life time and it is true during our lifetime. Jesus foresaw that it would be tough to follow him.

Some of the triumphalism and slogans that have come from Western Christendom are a disservice to Jesus and his gospel. Especially when the slogans tie up with political jargon. It is not surprising then that political and religious powers react when we come up with slogans such as 'India for Christ.'

Even when there are great revivals of the Spirit and major turning to Christ it does not follow that whole nations turn to Christ. Revivals impact nations and society. Revivals make nations great. But it does not follow that nations become Christian because of that.

This is why we were not party to the conversion propaganda of about 15 years ago which claimed about 300 million Dalits were turning to Christianity.

In fact we respected the choice of some Dalit leaders who chose other faiths as it was about freedom of religion and their free choice. It was Dr. B.R. Ambedkar who taught them to exercise their right to religion and freedom of conscience.

But we were also clear that we would accept all those who chose Jesus out of their own free will. We could not reject them due to fear or threats. We would not turn away the Dalits if they turned to the love of Christ. We would not dare to state by our action or words that they were not welcome by Jesus Christ as equal human beings.

We have seen how the Spirit of God has filled the lives of the masses and drawn them to Jesus Christ. We have seen the Spirit calling us to love people as whole persons. We have seen women touched and empowered by the love of Christ. It is true that many have found the amazing transforming love of Christ. They have experienced healing and deliverance and the presence of God.

The Good Shepherd Church of India does not believe in nor support any forced or fraudulent conversions. It believes that the regeneration about which the Bible talks is not a human activity. Inner regeneration is between the individual and Jesus Christ. It is a spiritual experience that defies any human manufactured program or method. It does not matter if such a person calls himself Christian or not as long as he confesses that he is a follower of Christ as Lord.

We insist that we will not tolerate a racist and casteist ideology in the Good Shepherd Church movement. Casteism is a problem in the religions of India including Christianity. Casteism has destroyed the development and growth of India.

We insist that Jesus came to bring healing and salvation to the whole person and whole communities. We do not treat people as disembodied souls. Too often by limiting the gospel to only about going to heaven we have allowed those who come to Christ to continue in their present hell.

The present hell refers to remaining as victims of slavery, caste, exploitation, crime and sin.

We believe that Jesus announced that in him the Kingdom of heaven had now come to earth. That there is a present fulfillment of this now and there is a future fulfillment in the full coming of the Kingdom of heaven.

The Good Shepherd Church is a home-grown Indian movement that links itself to 2,000 years of Christian faith and tradition. It celebrates that Jesus has been in the nation for 2,000 years. It is Indian and it is national. It is also global.

We dream of the Church reflecting the Kingdom of God in its full glory. The Kingdom of God touching every area of life. The body, the mind, the spirit and society are all areas of Kingdom concern for us.

The cause of Dalit Freedom has taught us much. We know that in as much as we love and empower the least of these, we do it unto Jesus as well.

The cause of girls and women in sexual slavery and debt bondage has opened our eyes to the fact that we humans make hell for others. Our work in freeing and rehabilitating those who are exploited continues strong. We especially work among those girls and women who are victims of ritualized prostitution.

It is hard to grasp that the majority people still do not know or understand the life and teachings of Christ. When they hear about him or see his life (for example through the *Dayasagar®* movie), they begin to glimpse who Jesus is.

Thus, Good Shepherd congregations across India continue to act as light and salt in their societies. They continue to see the mighty working of the Spirit in their midst. There are signs and wonders.

There is transformation of community life. There is the freeing of trafficked and enslaved women. Children get English medium education.

Mahatma Gandhi said if only Christians in India lived like Jesus Christ there would be no need to preach: Indians would follow Christ. Gandhi also said that if Jesus came in the flesh today he would own the allegiance of more people than others because of who he was when he lived on earth.

It is our desire that more and more people would find the Person of Christ through our lives and words through the Good Shepherd Church.

INTRODUCTION

This small book would never have been written if not for the rise of the Hindutva ideology and its proponents' incessant attacks against Christians which began in the late 1990s. Hate literature, false propaganda and physical attacks on Christian workers and churches, and the harassment of the State forced us to ask: Why did the Hindu extremists target Indian Christians? Why this hate culture and why the burning of Graham Staines and his sons in 1999?

Christians lived as peaceful citizens in the country and were not involved in any communal clashes or violent activities. Our neighbors loved us and we continue were as patriotic and nationalistic as any other Indian. In fact, a 2007 article in the Times of India newspaper published a BBC survey showing Indian Christians to be the most patriotic community in India.

As a Christian leader with over 40 years' experience in all kinds of compassionate Christian work across the nation, and as someone who has networked with all branches of Christianity in India and in other parts of the world, I knew of no evidence of the false propaganda accusing Christians of engaging in forced and fraudulent conversions. If anything, Christian workers were quietly carrying on their faithful, compassionate activities and witness to Christ.

As an Indian Christian leader who has stood for the independence and autonomy of the Indian Church in global Christian forums, it was strange for me to experience the insinuation that we were tools in the hands of some foreign powers.

Like my compatriots, I love being an Indian. I love India, its culture and its way of life. India is a great nation. I love our vast and diverse heritage. I admire the nation building process that has been going on since Independence in which Indian Christians, along with others, have played a major role. I support the Indian identity of all the diverse cultural groups within the Indian nation.

Yet there has been a systematic campaign of hate and attack hatched against us by the Sangh Parivar. As we researched the persecution against Christians, it became apparent that it was not primarily about us. It was about the Dalits. It was about the Bahujans. India has been in major caste turmoil for the last couple of decades. This upheaval has changed the social and political landscape of the nation.

There is no question about it. Many of the Dalits and Bahujans want out of the heinous caste system. Politicians have not delivered. Dalit atrocities are mounting by the day. In many places, the State is a mute spectator. What is written in the Constitution does not work itself out in the villages and towns of India where Dalit women are raped, abused, tortured, paraded naked and humiliated. In a previous BJP President's village in Andhra Pradesh, Dalits cannot drink water from the same well as the upper castes.

Thus began many meetings and discussions with Dalit-Bahujan leaders in the late 1990s. These meetings took place all across the nation and we Christians were immersed immediately into the Dalit-Bahujan struggle. Our mentors and teachers were now Dalit-Bahujan leaders and intellectuals. They were not Christians. We listened to them. We repented before them for caste discrimination within the Indian Church. Dalit-Bahujan leaders continue to talk to us and advise us.

We began to see why Christians are one of the greatest threats to the Hindutva brigade: we will welcome the Dalits into the body of Christ. That is the nature of Christ's teaching. If Dalits choose freely to turn to our faith, we will not reject them. If they want help, we will not turn them away. The Dalits and the OBCs have lost out spiritually, socially and developmentally in the last 50 years, not to mention what has happened to them in the past 3,500 years. A tiny minority continues to enjoy the riches, wealth and privileges of India. This minority rules and manages the richest temples of India and controls the nation's temple economy, one of the economic power centers of

Indian society.

Brahmanism's caste ideology helps them maintain their socio-spiritual monopoly. The casteist Hindutva movement is aimed at duping the Dalit-Bahujan people further. Dalit-Bahujan recruits are used to kill Christians, Muslims and others who do not subscribe to the Hindutva agenda. Christians and Muslims are portrayed as "enemies."

Hindutva subscribers in the West who enjoy the wealth and fruit of Western democracies send money to finance the Sangh Parivar and to keep Brahmanism alive.[1]

We realized that if we stayed silent, we would be silenced forever. We realized that we had to join the Dalit-Bahujan struggle for socio-spiritual freedom and liberation by using all non-violent means to fight those responsible for the oppression of the vast majority of Indians. This is why Christians are the greatest threat to Hindutva.

The struggle is far from over. Only when the Dalit-Bahujan peoples become socio-spiritually free, live with equal dignity, and are masters of their own fate and destiny in their own nation, will the struggle be over.

This book is just a small introduction to this complex phenomenon that besets my great nation.

There are many who have made this book possible and I want to express my thanks to all of them. I especially owe a lot of gratitude to Dalit-Bahujan intellectuals and leaders who have instructed me. My deepest gratitude also goes to the progressive upper caste leaders, especially the women, who encouraged me to take a proactive stand on this issue and not be intimidated by the Hindutva forces. A special thanks also to my colleague, K. Lajja, who helped in drafting this manuscript.

May the Dalits achieve Freedom — Now and Forever.

Joseph D'souza
Hyderabad, India
October 20, 2004

NOTES ON TERMS
AND CONCEPTS

Ambedkar, Dr. B.R.: Hailing from central India in the early 1900s, Ambedkar is known as the champion of the Dalits. Dr. Ambedkar was born into one of the lowest sectors of the Dalit caste hierarchy. Overcoming the many educational obstacles facing Dalits, he received his M.A., Ph.D., D.Sc., and L.L.D. in Law from Colombia University, USA, and London. Additionally, he received a D.Lit. from Osmania University in Hyderabad, India. He is known as the Father of the Indian Constitution. The Dalit movement for socio-spiritual freedom began with him. He was driven from one school to another, was forced to take classes outside the classroom, and was thrown out of hotels in the dead of night because he was considered untouchable.

Aryans: The word 'Aryan' means 'royal' or 'noble.' The Aryan people are fair in complexion. When they arrived in India more than 3,000 years ago, they considered themselves racially superior to all others, including the original inhabitants of India (the Dravidians and the aboriginals). They were responsible for the present caste system and the practice of untouchability in India.

Bahujan: Bahujans are considered the oppressed communities within the caste system. They are known as the low or backward castes, and though theoretically higher in socio-spiritual status than the Dalits, they do not enjoy equal rights or privileges with the upper castes.

Brahma: Brahma is one of the members of the chief Hindu godhead consisting of three main gods (the other two being Vishnu and Shiva).

While millions of other gods are worshiped within Hinduism, these three compose the main triumvirate in the Hindu scriptures and are generally considered most powerful and important. Brahma was the first god and Hindus consider him the God of gods.

Brahmin: Not to be confused with Brahma (one of the gods of Hinduism). The Brahmin people are the priestly class, the highest of the four divisions in ancient Hindu society. Strictly speaking, a Brahmin is one who knows and repeats the Vedas (Hindu scriptures). Brahmins conduct all the ritual affairs of Hindu society.

Buddhism: A religion founded by Gautama Buddha who was from a ruling caste (Kshatriya). He vehemently fought against Brahmanism's domination in the religious sphere and caste injustice in society.

Caste: According to Hinduism, people are innately divided into four groups called castes or varnas. The groups are Brahmin (the priestly caste); Kshatriya (the warrior caste and protectors of Hinduism); Vaishya (the business community); and Sudra (the supportive workers serving the three upper castes). Considered unclean and even lower in status than animals, the Dalits do not belong to this pyramid of castes and are therefore known as outcastes. The Brahmins comprise less than five percent of the total population, but they have maintained domination of Indian power, politics and religion for thousands of years. This was true even during the British Raj.

Christianity: Christianity is a religion that has a spiritual democratic tradition and culture. Jesus is the source of its faith, culture and traditions.

Dalit: The root for the word 'Dalit' is found both in Hebrew and in Sanskrit. It refers to people who are socially, religiously, economically and politically oppressed, deprived and exploited in India. The word 'Dalit' is often used to describe a person who comes from any lower caste, even though technically authentic Dalits are kept outside the caste system as unworthy to enter the social and religious life of society. They are generally considered to be polluted socially, poor economically and powerless politically. They are not allowed to touch caste Hindus and are therefore treated as 'untouchables.' Dalits are found spread throughout the nation of India, South Asia and among the Indian diaspora around the world.

Dravidians: Dravidians are the original inhabitants of India, mainly dark in complexion. They lived in the northern part of India and were pushed southward by the Aryan invaders.

Fascism: A school of thought that established oppressive conditions all over the world.

Hindu: The word 'Hindu' is derived from the Sanskrit word 'Sindhu' (a river, more specifically, the Indus). The Persians in the fifth century BC called the Hindus by that name, identifying them as the people of the land of the Indus. The religion of the Hindu people was therefore known as Hinduism. Medieval Muslim scholars coined the term Hindu.

Hindutva: The philosophy of right-wing fundamentalist Hinduism. It believes that India is for Hindus and should be ruled only by Hindus. The Hindutva forces believe in inseparability of politics and religion. Minorities should abide by and live at the mercy or goodwill of the majority. The Hindutva regime would like to establish one race (Hindu), one culture (Hindu) and one religion (Hinduism) in the Indian sub-continent. All other religious groups are considered a minority. Brahmanism dominates Hindutva ideology.

Kshatriya: This is the second most powerful caste in India. It is the ruling caste. Their welfare depends upon their respect for the priestly caste (Brahmins).

Mulnivasi: The original inhabitants of India. This term is used to include Dalits, Backwards, Other Backwards, and those converted to Christianity, Islam or Buddhism in different phases of Indian history.

RSS: Rastriya Swam Sevak Sangh. This is a Hindu extremist organization with a wide Hindu network. They have appointed themselves the guardians of India and the Hindu religion. They vehemently oppose Christianity and other minority religions in India. They are responsible for the false propaganda and hate campaign against minorities in India. They believe in violence as a divine necessity. Therefore, they distribute weapons openly and freely.

Scheduled Castes (SC): The Scheduled Castes are the people who come from the lowest of the Hindu castes. They are non-tribal by heritage. Government records use this term to refer to the Dalits, even though technically Dalits are in reality kept outside the caste system.

Scheduled Tribes (ST): Scheduled Tribes are the aboriginals of India. They, too, are oppressed and exploited by the higher castes and are kept outside the caste system. Earlier they were considered the criminal tribes by the upper castes. Most of these people live in the mountain regions and forest zones of India (also called 'Adivasis'). The Scheduled Castes and Scheduled Tribes often come together to stand up for their rights, even though they are different by family heritage.

Sanskrit: Sanskrit is the historical language of the Hindu religion. It is the language of the elite and high caste Brahmins. Most of the Hindu scriptures were written in Sanskrit. The language is generally learned only by the priestly caste. According to Manu, the lawgiver, Dalits should not even hear the reading of the scripture in Sanskrit. If this happens, boiled lead should be poured into the offending Dalit's ears.

Sudras: Bottom of the four castes. Some sub-castes are not allowed to own land, thus considered 'Bahujans.'

Tribal: Tribals are the original people of India. Today they are forced to live in the jungles. They are exploited by the three upper castes. Also called 'Adivasis.'

Vaishya: Vaishyas are third in the order of the upper caste hierarchy. They are responsible for business within Hindu society. Mahatma Gandhi belonged to this caste.

VHP: Vishwa Hindu Parishad. This is one of the many Hindu extremist organizations within India and around the world. They are registered in the USA as a 501(c)3 organization. In India they are notorious for their hate campaigns against Christians, and for inciting communal violence. Money that is raised in the West is sent out to further their agenda in India. They have led the attacks on minorities such as Christians and Muslims in India. They are largely responsible for the false propaganda and hate campaign against the minorities in India. They are the ones who conducted mass murders in Gujarat and subsequently tried to justify their actions.

Untouchables: Untouchables are considered so unworthy by the upper caste echelon that they are not part of the caste system. Untouchables are forbidden from physically touching any member of any caste. Doing so would render the latter "unclean" by Hindu scriptural law. Thus, the Dalits are commonly known as "untouchables." Other varieties of untouchability include "unseeables" (those who cannot be seen by a caste person) and "unapproachables" (those who cannot come near to a caste person). Previously called "outcastes."

CHAPTER ONE

OCTOBER 15, 2002: THE EXCEPTION AND THE RULE

On October 15, 2002, six-year-old Latha was sitting on a straw mat on the floor of her first grade classroom in rural Andhra Pradesh, South India. The room was small, its sea-green-colored paint peeling off the walls as a result of that year's heavy monsoon rains. She and her classmates were staring at a chalkboard in that rented house repeating diligently after the teacher as she taught them the English alphabet.

Latha was the first person in her family to go to school. Her parents, completely illiterate, despite their ability and desire, chose to invest what little money they had in paying a small school fee so their daughter could attend the new school which had opened in their village that year. It was a special English-medium school run primarily for the Dalits, the 'untouchables,' of the area. Never before had anyone cared about the education of the children in this village, so when the school opened, the most unfortunate families rushed to enroll their young ones.

Latha, as a representative of more than 3,000 years of oppression and discrimination against the Dalits of India, the lowest of low in the Hindu caste system, was finally getting her chance at a bright future. She was getting the chance to find equality, dignity and human rights. Her life as a Dalit was about to be radically changed. She was going to school with teachers who filled the classroom with love and compassion. Latha was finally getting an education that would prevent her from becoming another child laborer.

In stark contrast, October 15, 2002, was also a significant

day for the Dalit community in another part of India. It is a story too cruel to imagine, too inhuman, yet shockingly true: Five Dalits were brutally murdered in Jhajjar, Haryana. These were people like Latha and her parents, people who took pride in the work they were allowed to do, despite the work's socially stigmatized reputation. These five Dalits worked desperately yet faithfully to support their loved ones, despite the fact that society was, in principle, against their existence, an existence which quickly would be snuffed out.

Why were they murdered? What was their crime? They had skinned a dead cow and transported the cowhide. Was this illegal? Was it an offense to society? Absolutely not. In fact, the skinning of cows and the transporting of cowhide is a traditional occupation for a sizeable number of Dalits. It is an occupation assigned to them by the caste into which they were born. These five Dalits were mercilessly murdered simply for fulfilling their role in a caste-based society. However, the casteist forces believed their own murderous act to be righteous, because they believed the Dalits had first killed the cow, a holy animal, before skinning it. In theory, Dalits may touch only a deceased cow, so as not to defile a live cow with their 'untouchability.'

Indian civil society was outraged at the news of these murders. The cries of injustice heard around the nation were spontaneous and widespread. Progressive Hindus raised their voices. In contrast, however, soon after the incident, Giriraj Kishore, the Vice President of the Vishwa Hindu Parishad ('VHP,' a fundamentalist organization promoting Hindutva values across India), celebrated the killing of these five Dalits. He proclaimed the life of a cow more valuable than the life of a human being; more valuable than the life of a Dalit.[1] Another Hindu religious leader said that people must learn to live in the caste into which they were born. The local government's response was lethargic. Once again, the caste monster had reared its ugly head.

The Dalits of the state of Haryana were shocked, angered and distraught. Moreover, they felt saddened because they knew this was not an isolated event.[2] Atrocities against Dalits are massively widespread. There is plenty of press to prove it.

Human Rights Watch reports, "Between 1994 and 1996, a total of 98,349 cases were registered with the police nationwide as crimes and atrocities against Scheduled Castes. Of these, 38,483 were registered under the 1989 Scheduled Castes/Tribes Atrocities Act. A further 1,160 were for murder, 2,814 for rape, and 13,671 for hurt. Given that Dalits are both reluctant and unable (for lack of police cooperation) to report crimes against themselves, the actual number of abuses is presumably much higher."[3]

These statistics are twenty years old. At this rate, 153 Dalits are being physically tortured every day; six every hour. Despite public sentiment around the world to the contrary, today the atrocities are rising in frequency and in intensity by the minute.

Historically, the Indian Government has made efforts to control atrocities against the Dalits.[4] Though the Constitution of India bans untouchability,[5] it does not outlaw the caste system. Though it bans discrimination based on caste, it has not eliminated the caste virus in Indian society. The caste system is so deeply ingrained in the Indian cultural worldview through thousands of years of reinforcement that these half-hearted attempts at granting equality have been largely ineffective.

The Indian Government also offers economic assistance to Dalits. In an effort to ease the Dalit plight, the Constitution instituted and guaranteed an economic/social system called "Compensatory Discrimination" or "Reservation." This system grants privileges to Dalits through 'reservations' (affirmative action-type benefits) in government-run schools, colleges and institutions. A percentage of government jobs and parliamentary[6] positions are reserved for the Dalit people.

These constitutional and economic concessions, though, face difficulty in practical application. Why? A combination of the social worldview, a lack of English-medium educated Dalits on hand for hire, and a caste-based bias by those filling positions available through affirmative action all work together to prevent the full success of the reservation system.

While in theory this welfare measure extended to the Dalits should help eliminate discrimination, in reality the Dalits continue to endure centuries-old oppression, struggling for their human rights. Society simply refuses to relinquish caste. Since its inception thousands of years ago, caste has been the dominant force binding India together into an oppressive culture and social system. And rather than fading into the past as an historical monument of centuries gone by, the caste system and its accompanying oppression continue to grow, both according to general public sentiment, as well as through official records of governmental organizations in India such as the National Commission on Scheduled Castes and the National Human Rights Commission.

According to police records published by the National Crime Records Bureau, "The year 2006 witnessed an increase of 3.6% as 26,127 cases reported in 2005 increased to 27,070 cases in 2006."[7] Despite this increase in the number of reported cases of violence against Dalits, a landmark study in 2006 of 565 villages in 11 states revealed that Dalits were prevented from entering police stations in 28% of the villages.[8] We have to wonder how many cases are not recorded each year due to caste-based intimidation and discrimination.

An even bigger issue is the lack of convictions and punishment for people who attack Dalits. One analysis in 2006 by the media said, "While out of the total cases, only one in five were disposed, out of the disposed cases, a mere 2.31% ended up in conviction. The number of acquittals is six times more than the number of convictions." [9] Many Dalits feel that filing a case with the police will only increase their problems in the community, require them to spend the little money they might have saved on attorneys, and involve court appearances for many years. Pursuing justice in the legal system is not worth it.

Besides crimes against Dalits, there is pervasive, severe discrimination in everyday social practice by both the local authorities, as well as upper caste communities. The comprehensive 2006 study mentioned above, published as the book *Untouchability in Rural India*, goes on to say that untouchability, or the practice of treating Dalits as less than human, was evidenced in all local state institutions. For example, this study states that in 38% of government schools, Dalit children were made to sit separately while eating. In 20% of the schools, Dalit children were not permitted to drink water from the same source as upper caste children. Thirty-three percent of public health workers refused to visit Dalit homes, and 24% of Dalits still did not get postal deliveries at home. Segregated seating for Dalits was found in 31% of self-help groups and cooperatives, and Dalits were denied access to polling booths, or forced to form separate lines in 12% of the villages surveyed.

One of the authors of this shocking study concluded, "Despite being charged with a constitutional mandate to promote social justice, various local institutions of the Indian-State clearly tolerate and even facilitate the practice of untouchability." After citing examples and statistics of how Dalits are degraded by their communities while trying to sell their crops or merely getting water for their homes, the researcher says, "Dalits are therefore not only disproportionately burdened with poverty to start with; caste discrimination in labor and consumer markets condemns them to lower wages with harder work in uncertain employment and restrictions on their access to natural resources as well as the markets for their products." He ends by saying, "With untouchability thus persisting unashamedly in state institutions like schools and police stations, in public spaces like temples and shops, in farms and markets, and in homes and hearts, the Dalit still lives in India waiting hopelessly, and sometimes in anger, for the long-betrayed dawn of equality." [10]

In February 2008, a study was conducted in 47 villages across the south Indian state of Tamil Nadu.[11] In general, Tamil Nadu is applauded for its good education system and government efforts to alleviate discrimination against lower castes. However, the study, conducted by the Tamil Nadu Untouchability Elimination Front (TNUEF), noted an unwritten rule that gives higher caste Hindus priority over Dalits in boarding buses in many areas, allows for the elimination of bus stops in Dalit communities, turns a blind eye to transport employees picking fights with Dalit passengers, and tolerates Dalits' banishment from bus shelters.

This study found that in many schools Dalit pupils were not allowed to share water with upper caste Hindus. To punish a disobedient Dalit boy, teachers would scold him by calling him by his caste name. If the teacher decided that the boy needed corporal punishment, the task of beating the errant student was assigned to another Dalit boy because the teacher did not want to touch the Dalit. The study also found a systematic refusal to admit Dalits in certain schools. Sadly, there is still more.

A February 2008 study found that Dalits were not allowed to own male dogs for fear that a "Dalit dog" may mate with an upper caste dog. In some villages, Dalits were required to hide from caste Hindus during temple celebrations. The 'two-glass system,' where Dalits and non-Dalits are served beverages in different cups, is still prevalent in many places. Further, the Tamil Nadu State government still makes announcements in villages by beating a drum and yelling the news. They employ Dalits for this job.[12]

In late 2007, a study on the "Discrimination in Food Security Program" conducted by University Grants Commission (UGC) chairman Sukhdeo Thorat and Joel Lee of Columbia University found rampant discrimination throughout India. The authors said, "With casteism heavily dominating the Public Distribution System (PDS), Dalits are not only denied access to food but are also made to pay more money for less quantity and are charged higher prices. Of the total 521 villages surveyed in five states — Uttar Pradesh, Bihar, Rajasthan, Tamil Nadu and Andhra Pradesh — almost 40 percent reported that Dalits were found to be receiving less quantity for the same price as compared to the upper caste. The common practice is to drop food and money from above to the cupped hands of the Dalits to avoid touching them. In some villages ... PDS dealers even hang a separating curtain in the shop window before having any dealings with the members of the Musahars — a Dalit community." [13]

Most of India's citizens live in rural villages. The Indian government has embraced a system of village councils having legal authority and power. In a 2007-2008 report on these village councils (called 'panchayats'), the government admitted the practice of untouchability continues. During panchayat meetings Dalits are required to sit separately and drink tea and water from separate glasses. Worse, there are examples of violent incidents in which Dalits have tried to assert their rights. [14]

A human rights organization visited India in early 2008 and encountered perhaps the world's worst job and most devastating atrocity against Dalit-Bahujans: manual scavenging. But more than just a degrading occupation, this is a role some Indian citizens are told they were born to do. There is no other option. The encounter, recounted below, occurred in a village in Andhra Pradesh near the highway between two 'hi-tech' cities, Hyderabad and Bangalore. [15]

Peddanna's (name changed) role in life is to collect human

feces from a dry toilet and carry this excrement to a dumping ground. Peddanna is part of the Thoti sub-caste among the Dalits. Thotis are supposedly born to do 'manual scavenging,' which is the cleaning of human waste by hand. Every morning, Peddanna and five colleagues carry their baskets through the village to the dry latrine (dirt and grass surrounded by a low wall). Once they arrive there, they scoop the human waste into baskets and carry it away, giving the higher caste members of the village a clean toilet. They use flimsy makeshift scoops. They have no gloves, masks or protective equipment. For others, the job is even worse because many dry latrines have cement floors from which the feces must be scraped meticulously.

Peddanna said, "If it is raining, when we put the basket on our heads, the [excrement] covers our bodies." Like many manual scavengers, he has reoccurring stomach problems and difficulty eating because of the lingering noxious odor. When some feces fell on his head recently, he complained about the conditions to an official at the local government office employing him. The official appeared surprised, and said, "You are a dirty man doing a dirty job; why are you worried about this?"

The village chief (called 'sarpanch') threatened to punish Peddanna and his colleagues by withholding their salary if they complained to the municipal authorities or anyone else. Other villagers avoid the manual scavengers and their families and they are treated as unclean. They cannot enter restaurants or many public places where they could be recognized. Even other Dalits despise them. Is it any surprise that Peddanna turns to homemade liquor to alleviate his sense of shame about his work? If he could choose another career he would, but society's pressure combined with a lack of resources forces him to take up his basket each morning.

Manual scavenging was banned in India by a 1993 law, but legislation passed in India's capital has had little impact in rural areas where most of the manual scavenging population lives. Authorities often do not enforce the law. Some may claim they have not heard about the law. But, even worse, the government authorities often perpetuate the problem.

The government has said there are only a few hundred thousand people in this occupation and claims to be helping retrain them for other occupations as they install modern toilets. Even though making these moderate claims, the opposite is actually the truth. The government itself utilizes the services of manual scavengers. A communal dry latrine exists in the Nizamabad District Court in Andhra Pradesh state. Further, a large number of manual scavengers are employed across India by the Indian Railways, which is owned by the government. One of the leading organizations trying to help the manual scavengers, Safai Karmachari Andolan, directly denies the government's figures, stating that there are actually up to 1.3 million manual scavengers. Almost without exception, they are all Dalits.

While the discussion about atrocities against Dalits could go on extensively, we turn our attention to those suffering perhaps most greatly through caste-bias: Dalit women. Quite possibly the most widespread atrocities are indeed borne by Dalit women who face both caste and gender discrimination.

In June 2008, the Centre for Dalit Rights and the Program on Women's Economic, Social and Cultural Rights finished field surveys in five Dalit communities in two districts of Rajasthan, a state in north India known for its magnificent palaces, pottery, colorful culture, and camel fairs. They were trying to assess the "exclusion and subordination" of Dalit women. The report's conclusion was simple: "Dalit women are restricted to the bottom of society, impoverished and invisible as citizens." One author said the only occupations available and traditionally allocated to Dalit women were those that no one else would prefer to do and concluded, "The fact-finding clearly demonstrates that in spite of various laws and schemes for Dalits, not much is being done on the ground to address the day-to-day hardships faced by Dalit women."[16]

The speaker of the Rajasthan state legislature was at the press conference when the report was released. She admitted that "systematic denial" of rights to education, training, land, and other resources has led to the exclusion of Dalit women from all socio-economic and political fields. According to media reports, she concluded, "Access to education will surely enable Dalit women to assert their rights and improve their living conditions."

But access to education is not a simple issue. In 2005, the Indian press highlighted the story of one female Dalit student. Mamata Nayak, fifteen years old, who lives in a village in the eastern state of Orissa. She was the first girl from her village to pass her exams and qualify for higher secondary education, and she enrolled in a college that was about four miles from her home. She decided to ride her bicycle to school, but a village through which she had to pass did not allow Dalits to ride bicycles or motorized vehicles on their roads and pathways. When she told her father that she would break the rule to get more education, he went to the village council. The village chiefs, mostly upper caste men, refused to change the law.[17]

The determined girl decided to ride her bike anyway, and walk it when she neared the village. However, the upper castes still threatened her. Eventually police had to assign an officer to accompany the girl on her daily commute.

Although these stories from Rajasthan and Orissa seem to be isolated events in different regions, the findings and stories ring true across India. Even international groups are beginning to see the clear evidence of caste and gender bias as they recognize and acknowledge the big picture portrayed in village after village across the nation.

On August 8, 1993, India finally ratified the United Nations Convention on the Elimination of All Forms of Discrimination Against Women of 1979 (a 14-year gap between passing of the Convention ruling and implementation within India). In February 2007, a committee monitoring the implementation of the principles represented by this UN Convention severely criticized India for its treatment of Dalit women. After reading reports by many non-governmental groups and considering responses by India's government, the committee said it was deeply concerned "about the ongoing atrocities committed against Dalit women and the culture of impunity for perpetrators of such atrocities."[18]

As mentioned, manual scavenging is one of many horrible occupations assigned to Dalits. What is not widely recognized is that most manual scavengers are women. In May 2008, a study in New Delhi, India's capital, revealed that about 80% of the city's 1,282 manual scavengers are women.[19] National estimates say 95% of manual scavengers are women.[20] The UN committee commented in its report that "despite a law banning manual scavenging, this degrading practice continues with grave implications for the dignity and health of the Dalit women who are engaged in this activity." The committee demanded that the Indian government help Dalit women by "putting in place modern sanitation facilities and providing the Dalit women engaged in this practice with vocational training and alternative means of livelihood."

As if being subjected to life as a manual scavenger were not enough, sexual abuse of Dalit women is another weapon used by the upper castes in many places. It is an ironic contradiction: Dalits are viewed as untouchable except when it comes to exploitative sexual relations. From rape to prostitution, this is the worst type of paradox. Human Rights Watch documented in a report to the UN examples of the upper castes using gender violence to intimidate Dalits. But, tragically and inexcusably, police have abused Dalit women in numerous incidents.[21] A human rights report by the U.S. State Department included graphic, tragic examples of upper caste gangs who used mass rape to intimidate lower castes.[22]

Partners of the Good Shepherd Church of India, the Dalit Freedom Network and the All India Christian Council, told all of this to the U.S. Congressional Human Rights Caucus during a briefing titled "Untouchables: The Plight of Dalit Women" on May 1, 2007. Ms. Smita Narula, Executive Director of the Center for Global

Human Rights and Global Justice at the New York University School of Law, and Mr. T. Kumar, Advocacy Director Asia and Pacific of Amnesty International, also supported our analysis with views of their own. Ms. Narula is widely-known for her unprecedented report "India's Broken People" which, when it was released by Human Rights Watch in 1999, drastically raised global awareness of the plight of the Dalits.[23] As she sat beside our delegation in Washington, D.C., she said, "The nature and frequency of violence against Dalit women serves to highlight the incongruence between the reality of Dalit women's lives and the universal right of women to freedom from any gender-based violence that results in physical, sexual, or psychological harm. Such violence also stands as a strong indictment of the failure of the Indian government to respect, protect and ensure Dalit women's rights. Statistics on the frequency of these crimes, which themselves grossly underestimate the pervasiveness of the abuse, reveal a culture of violence and impunity that rob Dalit women of their rights to security and basic human dignity."[24]

In addition to all of the abovementioned forms of oppressive activity against Dalits — both men and women in rural India, urban India also is experiencing caste bias, though "India's Shining" claims of globalization and tolerance try to paint the picture otherwise. As Dalits across the nation take advantage of whatever affirmative action benefits they can find and as some Dalits beat the odds to obtain a valuable English-based education, Dalits in urban India are experiencing new forms of discrimination which are not as obvious as adhering to the "two-cup system," cleaning human feces, or receiving a beating by an upper caste village chief. Instead, there are allegations that many Dalits are disqualified by Human Resources Departments in multinational corporations when they spot Dalit-heritage family names on applications and in interviews. Indeed, a two-year study by researchers at the Indian Institute of Dalit Studies and Sociologists supported by Princeton University's Institute for International and Regional Studies confirmed this growing phenomenon.[25] Some Dalits have complained there is a glass ceiling when it comes to promotions. Others simply note the "don't ask, don't tell" policy employers seem to have when it comes to the topic of caste.

⚜

And now we return to the beginning of our story. The five Dalits mentioned at the beginning of this chapter who were murdered for skinning a dead cow on October 15, 2002, were victims of centuries-old oppression. They lived and died the reality of the caste situation in India today. Untouchability is illegal, but as we have clearly seen, the ramifications of caste still live strong. The treatment of these young men is the rule of the day.

Young Latha, however, the girl we met in the small Dalit village in Andhra Pradesh, sits in stark contrast to the murdered Dalits of Jhajjar, in a classroom learning in an English-medium school. She is the exception to society's rule. Somehow, her destiny has led her to a place where she will have an escape from the tyranny of caste. She will have the chance to experience a future that does not include skinning cows, that does not include cleaning excrement from the city streets, that does not include selling her body for sexual favors to one day put food on the table for her own young children.

Imagine that four years later we meet young Latha once again. This time, she is standing next to her father at a community 'city hall' meeting in her village. The community is having a heated discussion over land prices and property taxes. The visiting officials who have come to offer consultation on the matter do not know the language of the village and Latha's father is struggling to make his point as he stands before the city council arguing his case.

It is then that Latha speaks up. She speaks in perfect English to the visiting officials and helps to negotiate the matter for her father and the other villagers present that day. Her young yet confident voice echoes through the crowded hall as her four years of English-based education are put to the test. Latha is a Dalit girl. But Latha now speaks English. Latha represents India's oppressed majority who are standing on the precipice of full life transformation.

Latha is the 'exception.' However, because of stories like the Dalits who were murdered in Haryana and thousands of other equally mortifying atrocities, the call to Dalit Freedom is ringing clearly across the nation of India and around the world. It is for this reason that the world and the Dalit community must know that Jesus loves the Dalits, the poor and the marginalized peoples across India. The Good Shepherd Church of India exists to offer the Dalits freedom in Jesus Christ.

CHAPTER TWO
JESUS AND BRAHMANISM

Jesus Christ loves the Dalits. His teachings promote human dignity and self-worth, and His compassion is powerful enough to make a lasting difference in the lives of those who follow Him. The Good Shepherd Church of India offers this love in Jesus to the poor and marginalized and seeks for them full life transformation. However, expressing the truth of God's love to the Dalits has never been easy. Brahmanism and its inherent cultural and socio-spiritual strength always seem to interfere.

Mahatma Phule pointed out 150 years ago that British Christianity in India was not living up to the teachings of Christ even as it allowed Brahmanism's forces to interpret both India and caste-based Hinduism. In his book Slavery, Phule attacked the British powers for withdrawing the teachings of the Bible from Indian schools. This curriculum had become a source of teaching on human equality and spiritual democracy. It was destined to make a positive difference in Indian society. However, the British rulers could not withstand the pressure applied by Brahmanism in the state of Maharashtra, and withdrew the teachings of the Bible from the classrooms.

Mahatma Phule correctly stated that the teachings of Jesus would unleash powerful forces of socio-spiritual liberation movements within Dalit-Bahujan communities in India. Caste-based discrimination, oppression and victimization cannot derive any support from what Jesus taught and from what He did on the Cross.

On the Cross, Jesus became the ultimate victim of injustice, facing the abuse of both religious and state power. Those who victimized Him could not tolerate Jesus' idea that all human beings

are equal before God, that God created no inherent difference
between the races, and that He allows all people to have equal
liberation, equal salvation, equal opportunities and equal blessings
from Him. He smashed the notion of human mediators between
God and the common people. He spoke against the monopoly of the
priestly class in religious matters. In short, Jesus' message and life
were a complete antithesis to Brahmanism.

At the Cross, spiritual fascism was dealt a death blow as
spiritual rights were extended to all people freely and equally; namely,
the right of access to God in this life through forgiveness of sins, the
right of free access to places of worship, and the right of access to the
priesthood for all. Jesus demolished once for all the social and racial
boundaries that divided people. He inaugurated a new humanity,
a new community on earth. The Cross condemns and rejects
discrimination based on race, descent or religion.

At the Cross, Jesus ensured the full and final victory of
all victims. His death signaled victory over oppressive forces of
victimization, both spiritual and physical. Simply put, at the Cross,
Jesus the crucified, innocent victim was declared Lord of all. God
gave all power to the Ultimate Victim. Ever since Jesus' crucifixion,
the voice of this Victim refuses to be silenced in world history. He
became Savior and Lord of the human race by dying, not by killing.

The Cross has had tremendous impact on the course
of history as victims of all oppression have found impetus and
inspiration to carry on their struggle for freedom and justice through
non-violent means. Death itself is no more an object of fear in order
to achieve spiritual freedom, liberation and justice. Jesus generates
courage and confidence in death and in suffering.

The Cross of Christ is the place of forgiveness, shelter,
liberation, acceptance and hope for Dalits and all the oppressed.
The Cross of Christ is also the place where Brahmanism meets its
judgment and condemnation.

Who would have thought that Jesus' struggle with the
religious leaders of his day, the Pharisees and the Sadducees, would

parallel so closely the struggle against Brahmanism? The Pharisees as a religious class exhibited most of the features of the Brahmanism of India, which are the same characteristics against which Ambedkar and others so fiercely fought. Consider the following points of similarity.

First, Jesus refused to ban anyone from access to God and the temple. When the Samaritan woman met Jesus she was astonished that Jesus would actually talk to her. She was an untouchable of her day. She could not go to the temple where she thought she could meet and worship God. She was considered a polluted sinner, yet Jesus reached out to her. He accepted her and let her know that God would forgive all her sins and completely embrace her. Her background (i.e., her caste) was not a barrier since she was a child of God like everyone else. This personal interaction with Jesus completely changed the Samaritan woman's life.

Brahmanism continues to insist on the notion that only the priestly caste has access to the main temples and to God, and that Brahmins are the highest form of human life because of their inborn purity. The Dalits and the Backward Castes do not have this status and thus are destined to a life with no real access to God.

Second, Jesus mingled with the dregs of society, the poor, the sinners and those who were considered polluted. The Pharisees simply could not digest that Jesus, who claimed to be the Son of God, would deliberately mix with the publicans, sinners, outcasts and rejects of society. He met with them, dined with them, and talked to them about the coming new Kingdom of God.

The Pharisees and Sadducees, like those who follow Brahmanism, had made their own ideas about which human beings were pure, righteous and acceptable to God, and which human beings were not. The Pharisees dared not mix with polluted people or be seen in their company.

Jesus fiercely challenged this attitude with His new vision of the Kingdom in which all people are made in the image of God and in which the God of love reaches out to the oppressed, the poor, the sinners and the downtrodden. This concept of the Kingdom of God is directly opposed to the tenets of Brahmanism preordaining people based on sins committed in a past life, condemning them to a caste prison forever.

Third, Jesus introduced and emphasized the concept of God as the Father of all. In direct contrast with Pharisaic teaching and Brahmanism, Jesus taught that God was actually the Father of all human beings. This means we all come from one Father God. None of us come from His feet and none of us are the unborn or the untouchable. There is no such thing as a preordained hierarchy of human beings.

The Pharisees and Sadducees, like Brahmanism's teachers, found this doctrine tormenting. Suddenly, in the new Kingdom of God, Jesus pronounced there was equality for all of us in relation to God. Jesus stated that every human being was an equal child of God and could authentically call God His Father. When the Pharisees saw that Jesus was eating with the outcasts and tax collectors, they asked His disciples, "Why does He eat with such people?" Jesus heard them and answered, "People who are well do not need a doctor, but only those who are sick. I have not come to respectable people, but outcasts" (Mark 2:17).

Fourth, Jesus rejected the notion that some people face today's oppression because of sins committed in a past life. At one time Jesus' disciples asked Him about a man who was disabled. They wondered whether it was because the man was more sinful than others. Jesus rejected this concept because Jesus knew that in God's eyes we are all equally sinners who need His love, grace and forgiveness. God knows no man is perfect. He knows that no Brahmin or Pharisee is less of a sinner than any other person in the human race.

Jesus clearly taught that God was completely impartial and did not have favorites. Jesus' main goal was to embrace the oppressed, the poor, the needy, and the sinful, all of whom look to Him for grace, help and forgiveness.

Jesus completely rejected the notion that our fate in this life is determined by sins in a past life. He rejected the idea of a past life altogether. He clearly emphasized that our entire existence is based solely on the present life and the life to come in the Kingdom of God.

Fifth, Jesus refused the notion that man needs a human mediator to connect with God. Through their teaching and resulting lifestyle, the Pharisees and Sadducees earned money and power by becoming mediators between God and man. Brahmanism also thrives on this teaching. Thus, India has a temple economy and a politicized religion.

Jesus told the Samaritan woman and others that through Jesus, God is available to every human being in his own heart. Mankind does not need a human mediator. Jesus, through His death on the Cross, shattered the need for a human mediator by becoming the Ultimate Mediator, the Ultimate Priest. Once for all, through achieving the acceptance of God and the forgiveness of sins, man can approach God directly in his heart. There is no need for temple sacrifice. No need to bribe God.

By teaching this ideology and then insisting on its application, Jesus shook the very foundation of the Pharisaic religious system. The Pharisees realized that this teaching was revolutionary and their days of power over people were numbered. The same teaching is a direct challenge to Brahmanism 2,000 years later. We do not need a priestly class to mediate between mankind and God. We can all have direct access to God. We can all become priests. In fact, we can all become the temple of God.

Sixth, Jesus taught that we should be loyal citizens, as well as loyal worshipers of God. The Pharisees and Sadducees, like Brahmanism today, tried to confuse the lines between the worship of God and the duties of the citizen to the State. One day they tried to trap Jesus by asking him whether it was right for people to pay taxes to the Government. Jesus' classic answer was that we should give to Caesar what is Caesar's and to God what is God's. No one should confuse the two. As citizens of any country, we should give to the nation all that the nation rightly requires of us. We should be patriotic and nation builders. We should work for development, peace and communal harmony. We should work for justice and righteousness.

At the same time, we should give to God what is God's. Only God deserves to be worshiped by human beings. Only God has the power to destroy or preserve our soul. Jesus saw no contradiction between the two realms.

However, Pharisaical teaching and Brahmanism both attempt to create this tension between faith and the State. Brahmanism's Hindutva project is designed to force us to agree with Brahmanism. They say those who do not agree are not true Indians, which is insidious teaching and propaganda.

Finally, Jesus' definition of true religion was different from Brahmanism's idea of religion. Jesus challenged the Pharisees and Sadducees on the nature of true religion. According to the Pharisees, it was all about wearing certain clothes, doing certain rituals, and following innumerable rules on purity and sacrifice. Further, religion was about words, more words, and religious festivals and events. Conversely, Jesus said true religion exists in the practice of faith. He said that faith without works of righteousness, justice and compassion was dead.

True religion is about taking care of those who are robbed and left on the road. True religion is about giving water to those who are thirsty. It is about providing food for the hungry, sight for the blind, care for the sick, and encouragement for the dying and bereaved. It is about cleaning the body of the leper, living with the untouchables of society, and bringing communities together. True religion is about being peacemakers rather than violence creators, standing up for the powerless in society, protecting the rights of women and children, joining hands with all those who are doing good, and standing in solidarity with the oppressed, the victimized and the forsaken. True religion in India is embracing the Dalits who have remained untouchable for centuries.

As we consider the above, we can see clearly why the perpetrators of Brahmanism have counted Jesus as their supreme enemy in India's current turmoil. Jesus was not bothered about the Pharisees and the Sadducees; He knew they would kill Him because of this. He was prepared to die. He knew this teaching was costly and would involve suffering. Just, righteous and non-violent revolutions are costly. Similarly, Jesus would not have bothered about the Brahminical and Hindutva forces. He is on a path to embrace all Dalits of India. He is on a course to sit with them and eat whatever is available in their huts.

As Jesus demonstrated with the Pharisees and Sadducees, all Indians must counter Brahmanism on an ideological basis. Like Jesus, who challenged Pharisaic religion, we should not be afraid to speak out on behalf of justice and truth. The main weapon we have is the truth and its power to dismantle all falsehood. This is the stand we are going to take and we are ready for whatever may come as a result.

If the upper caste leadership and even sections in the Church are irritated by our stand, so be it. We need to show great fortitude and courage. Like Jesus, we should intentionally mix with the Dalit-Bahujan community in our social and economic interaction. Our practice in daily life should challenge the inequities in our society.

Like Jesus, we should be non-violent in our challenge of Brahmanism. We cannot counter hate with hate or violence with violence. The oppressor is often the one who is in the most needy state because he can evolve into a human monster.

Brahmanism and extremist Hindutva forces killed the Father of the Nation, Mahatma Gandhi. Gandhi's life was impacted enormously by Jesus' Sermon on the Mount. He tried his best to reform the system and build a genuine sense of pan-Indian nationhood. The same Hindutva forces burned Australian missionary Graham Staines and his sons. The same forces engaged in genocide in Gujarat a couple of years ago.

Like Jesus, Gladys Staines, the widow of the martyred Graham who worked among the untouchables, openly forgave her husband's killers. Stephen, the first martyr of the Church, publicly forgave the Pharisees and other religious leaders of his day as they were killing him. Jesus stated on the cross, "Father, forgive them for they know not what they do."

Therefore, like Jesus, we must use the power of truth and justice, combining it with the power of love. Nothing can withstand this divine combination of forces.

Jesus knew, of course, that death was not going to be the end. He knew it was in His death and resurrection that He would carry His vision of the Kingdom of God into true and lasting fulfillment. In His resurrection, the Dalits of India will also resurrect. India as a nation is in the process of its ultimate rebirth toward greatness.

CHAPTER THREE
CASTE AND ITS CONSEQUENCES FOR THE DALITS

As we seek greatness for the nation of India and as we heed the call to Dalit Freedom in the Kingdom of God on earth today, we return to the plight of today's Dalits and the caste-based discrimination they face.

Let's journey to the center of the sub-continent. Nagpur, Maharashtra. The area is widely known as the crossroads of India. Located near the exact geographical center of the country, its culture is an easy blend of the North and the South, and the area is poised for massive global expansion as a mega-hub for transportation, communication and industry. This obvious attempt at globalization, however, has not stopped caste-based oppression from rearing its ugly head.

It had been a routine day for the Dalits of Khairlangi village outside Nagpur in September 2006. They had been going about their usual society-appointed professions, simply trying to provide food, clothing and shelter for their families. However, routine turned to tragedy for one Dalit family, the Bhotmanges. Without warning, assailants entered their home, attacked them, and left them to die, bleeding and broken. Why the attack? Mrs. Bhotmange had asserted her genuine legal right to her land and the upper castes did not like her boldness. As her penalty, she and her daughter were raped and died along with their son soon thereafter.

The response by the local police authorities was less than adequate. Public outrage ensued locally and nationally. Some financial and emotional compensation was given to the survivors, but nothing could bring back the dead or recompense the apathy of the high caste about this blatant act of caste-based aggression. The court case drags on.

The question remains: how can violent acts like this one, like the murders in Haryana, and like so many others from around the nation occur even today in the twenty-first century amid progressive movement in all nations of the world, including India and other areas of the Global South?

The answer? Caste. The Hindu caste system and its deeply ingrained worldview in India have permeated the depths of the human soul, allowing the continued discrimination. When did the caste system begin? How did it make such an indelible mark on Indian society? Caste was born out of Hinduism, one of the world's oldest and largest socio-religious belief systems.

According to widely accepted theory, Hinduism started as the union of three different religious traditions: Aryanism, the religion of the Aryans who worshiped Vishnu and came to India during the second millennium before Christ; Dravidianism, the religion of the Dravidians who worshiped Shiva; and Animism, the religion of the tribal people[1] who worshiped nature.

When the Aryans invaded India more than 3,500 years ago, they fought and subdued the native Dravidians and other original inhabitants. To maintain their purity of race, the Aryan invaders created their own social order and divided the community. This was, by many, the believed start of the caste system as we know it today in India.

The story of caste's origin, however, has been disputed by some. The best evidence is genetic and consequently undeniable. As stated, a large number of historians contest that the caste system has its origins in the Aryan conquest of India. The Aryans constructed caste ideology as a religious, political and social tool to rule the original inhabitants of the land. The extremist Hindutva forces that are committed to the perpetuation of the caste system have disputed this thesis most recently.

In modern days, and after decades of research, the Human Genome project analyzing the DNA composition of humans has produced scientific evidence stating that the genetic origin of the upper castes in India is more European than Asian.

What follows is the main result of the research as carried out by Utah University in collaboration with Andhra University and others:

"Analysis of these data demonstrated that the upper castes have a higher affinity to Europeans than to Asians, and the upper castes are significantly more similar to Europeans than are the lower castes. Collectively, all five datasets show a trend toward upper castes being more similar to Europeans, whereas lower castes are more similar to Asians. We conclude that Indian castes are most likely to be of proto-Asian origin with West Eurasian admixture resulting in rank-related and sex-specific differences in the genetic affinities of castes to Asians and Europeans."

This genetic evidence supports the long held view that caste slavery was constructed by foreigners who entered India and who created an elaborate social and spiritual system to dominate and rule the original inhabitants of the land. This genetic finding is no less important than the other finding stating that all human beings have come from one pair of original parents.

Whether genetic or merely socio-political in its origin, as time passed, the caste system's social order gained Hindu religious sanction. The Manusmriti book of Hindu holy legal code outlined the social order governing Hindu society. This society was divided into four castes.[2] Each caste, as theologically explained by the Vedas (the Hindu scriptures), allegedly descended from a specific part of the body of the Hindu god, Brahma. The three upper castes (Brahmins, Kshatriyas, Vaishyas) now make up 15 percent of the population and were taken from the head, the arms/shoulder and the belly/thigh of Brahma, respectively.

The highest caste, the Brahmins, make up approximately four percent of the total population of India. This minority still holds most of the power in the nation, as they have for thousands of years. The Sudras, or the Slave castes (today called the Backward Castes and comprising 50-52% of the population), were said to have come from Brahma's feet. Of the total population, an estimated 16-25% are 'untouchables' and 'tribals' (also called 'adivasis') who do not belong to any of the four castes. The Aryans deemed their professions (i.e., tanning of leather, sweeping the streets, or cleaning and carrying human excrement) unclean. Society shunned these people along with the so-called 'criminal tribes,' a terminology used to position the Tribals of India. The aboriginal tribals constitute about eight percent of the population. The remaining members of society belong to the minority religions like Islam, Christianity, Sikhism and Buddhism.

While the Vedas set forth the theological basis for the caste system, it was Manu, the Hindu lawgiver, who codified the strict caste rules rationalizing the oppression of Dalits and women today. Manu's rules reduced the Dalits to be worth less than animals, making them objects of abuse, exploitation and oppression.[3] These caste rules bound the Dalits to degrading manual labor under the regime of the upper castes. Dalits accepted their fate, believing they had done unspeakable acts in previous lives, that God did not love them, that they were born to serve the upper castes, and that they had no rights.

Manu's rules implemented these allegedly divine tenets on a practical level. Temple entry, for instance, is prohibited for the Dalits and Sudras. (The lower castes are allotted their own gods, goddesses and festivals.) They cannot come in contact with those of a higher caste. Even stray dogs can enter freely into the presence of upper caste men and women, but the Dalits cannot. Though scripted thousands of years ago, these tragic conditions continue to exist, even today, for India's Dalits.

Mahatma Gandhi, in an effort to rectify the situation, called Dalits 'Harijans' meaning 'the children of God.' However, Gandhi's unwillingness to tackle the whole issue of the caste system rather than merely its symptoms led the Dalits to distance themselves from the term Harijans, which today is seen as derogatory. Dr. John Dayal of the All India Christian Council gives reference to the origin of the word 'Harijan': "The term Harijan means literally, 'people of Hari,' one of the Hindu trinity. In common use it means 'children of God.' Originally Narsi Mehta of Gujarat used this term for the Dalit people. It was census time during the British regime. They wanted to give communal representation to the Dalits. However, the census officers faced a problem. There were many thousands of Dalit children who did not know the name of their fathers. These children were born of mothers forced into temple prostitution. The dominant caste men would use such 'dedicated' Dalit women for sex inside the temples. Disparagingly, Narsi Mehta said it would be appropriate to call such Dalit children 'children of Hari' as they were born of sex that took place in the name of gods."[4]

The untouchables themselves have adopted the term 'Dalit' referring to a status or condition, not to caste position. 'Dalit'[5] is derived from a Sanskrit equivalent meaning 'crushed,' 'broken,' or 'downtrodden,' accurately reflecting the Dalits' desperate condition as they endure social, religious, economic and political oppression.[6]

It is with the origin of caste that the story and plight of India's Dalits commences. It is the story of girls like Latha from Chapter One, of the men who were murdered in Haryana, and of the family killed in Nagpur. It is the story of human beings, just like millions around the world, who face massive discrimination because of their family heritage and the stigma assigned to them from a system both socially and religiously sanctioned by a small minority. This oppressive history has lent itself to incredible present day bondage, terror and atrocity.

India's Dalits number approximately 250-300 million men,

women and children. Because Dalits are deemed low and backward in the social and religious structures of society, they are denied not only spiritual rights, but also basic human rights. They are commonly refused entry to public parks and temples. Use of public wells is denied, and many restaurants keep separate drinking glasses or clay cups for Dalit use.[7] Only two to three percent of Dalit women can read and write. Millions of Dalit children serve as bonded laborers. The UN International Labor Office states, "… the overwhelming majority of bonded labor victims in agriculture, brick making, mining and other sectors are from the Scheduled Castes [or Dalits]."[8] The Economist's "The World in 2007" edition reports, "[Bonded labor] is widespread in India … Entire families may be enslaved in this way; usually they are low-caste or 'untouchable'."[9]

Dalit-Bahujan children are used as domestic servants, sweeping floors, washing dishes, and cleaning toilets, all while being kept out of school and being paid only a paltry sum of less than US $10 per month. The illiteracy rate among Dalit adults and Dalit children is alarmingly higher than the national average. Many Dalit villages have a literacy rate of only 10-20%, while the national average is around 50% and growing.

While many Dalit-Bahujan children and their parents choose domestic labor over education for purely economic reasons, some Dalit children are forced into the heinous crime that is child labor. Government figures say there are about 12.6 million child laborers in India, but child rights activists say the number is closer to 60 million.[10] Further, if the definition of child labor includes children under 14 years old who are not attending school and likely participating in unorganized sector jobs (i.e., subsistence farming), then the number of children involved in labor increases to 100 million nationwide.[11]

The government passed laws to stop child labor in the late 1980s, but only implemented the legislation in October 2006.[12] Despite this loosely applied legislation, the realities and heart-wrenching stories of ruined Dalit lives remain hidden.

The reality? Millions of Dalit children are involved in hazardous, life-threatening industries. Such occupations include carpet weaving, glass and bangle manufacturing, gem stone cutting, matchstick and fireworks production, and more. These jobs expose children to hazardous chemicals, unhealthy working conditions, and dangerous activities. While Dalits make up nearly one-fourth of India's general population, a study found that Dalits represent about 62% of the employees of six "hazardous" industries in three states of India. If other oppressed communities, which are usually included under the umbrella term "Dalit-Bahujan," are considered, then the total is close to 90%.[13] Sadly, reports of verbal and sexual abuse are highest among Dalit and lower caste children.[14]

About half of India's child laborers are modern day slaves. Forced or "bonded" child laborers number about 15 million. For most of them, their parents took a loan for the basic necessities of life and could not repay it. As a result, the children are forced to work to pay off the loan. Their wages are so small, though, that even after decades of backbreaking work, the loan cannot be repaid.

Young Manjula (name changed) is one such Dalit child ensnared in the slavery of bonded child labor. From the age of four, this child accompanied her mother in the pre-dawn hours to the matchstick production factory in Sivakasi, Tamil Nadu. Forsaking sleep, forsaking safety, she and her mother worked in hazardous, disgusting conditions, for just a few Rupees a day. They watched every month as dozens of their 'colleagues' received chemical burns and life-altering injuries from explosions. They lived in fear of the work environment and of physical abuse from their supervisors if they did not meet the daily production quota.

Today, Manjula is 12 years old. Sadly, her younger sister, Kavitha, has also been forced to enter into matchstick production. Her parents live in a never-ending cycle of debt. Manjula and Kavitha are the collateral with which those debts will be repaid. With scars on their frail, undernourished bodies to tell the tale, these girls have been denied a childhood; denied a life of freedom.

As previously mentioned, the consequences of caste for Dalit women are especially cruel and dehumanizing. Dalit women are frequently abused and sold into local prostitution and the larger sex trade across Asia, even expanding beyond India's borders. Through the efforts of domestic and international advocacy agencies, the world is learning about the plight of Dalit women and some are trying to take action.

A small NGO based in the state of Bihar in Eastern India publicizes the reality of life as a Dalit woman. A report called 'Bojh' released by Bhoomika Vihar in 2006 stated that approximately 98% of women and girls being trafficked belong to Scheduled Castes, Other Backward Castes and minorities.[15] The survey only covered a small region, but most experts believe the statistics are true when extrapolated nationally. The US State Department noted Bhoomika Vihar's work in its annual report on human rights for 2006. "Traffickers usually targeted minors and Dalit women (for the sex trade)," said the US State Department Country Reports on Human Rights Practices, 2006.

In a recent compendium by the UK's Jubilee Campaign, written by Danny Smith, one full chapter is given to the story of the modern-day slavery that is human trafficking and the sex trade. In this book, published mid-2007, I had the privilege of showing the true extent to which Dalit women face abuse and oppression. I wrote the story of Premila (name changed), a Dalit woman from a small village in rural Bihar, who had been captured into India's sex trade. On Premila's eighteenth birthday, her parents, who had suffered the shocking cruelties of a Dalit existence, signed their daughter over to a nightmare. For the negligible sum of 800 Rupees (~US $13), she was sold to a man living in the state of Punjab. He claimed there were no 'good women' in his village and therefore he was forced to purchase a wife. 'Wife' is a loose term. 'Sexual slave' would be more accurate. Premila became a modern-day concubine. Her body was used and abused at the will of this man, her 'husband,' and of any of his male relatives who came to call. It was a living hell. Eventually, a new 'investment opportunity' presented itself and Premila was turned out of her new 'family' in Punjab and sold to a well-known prostitution ring in the nation's capital, New Delhi. The sex trafficking trade runs rampant there and Premila brought a relatively good price: 5,000 Rupees (~US $80). She joined thousands of other women who exist in impoverished, disease-ridden, dangerous conditions. She was forced to surrender her body under threat of abuse or death.

Premila was a 'good' employee and was traded yet again to the streets of Mumbai for 35,000 Rupees (~US $570). It was here that she was finally rescued by a domestic NGO/aid agency. Returned to her hometown in Bihar, she was a broken woman. She will never re-marry. She will likely die young; used, abused and forgotten.

The consequences of caste produce a list of atrocities against Dalit men, Dalit women, and Dalit children that could go on and on. The US State Department Country Reports on Human Rights Practices 2006 highlights, "Upper caste gangs at times used mass rape to intimidate lower castes, and there were reports of gang rape as punishment for alleged adultery or as a means of coercion or revenge in rural property disputes." Chandra Bhan Prasad's latest book, "Dalit Phobia: Why do they hate us?" produces the following outrageous occurrences.[16]

> Gohana, Haryana. September 2005: Only 62 miles from Delhi, the nation's capital, upper caste men with tractors destroy and burn 60 Dalit houses. This was due to a fight between a Jat (upper caste man) and

local Dalit youth.

Jhabbar, Punjab. January 2006: Bant Singh, a Dalit farm laborer and activist, was beaten by upper caste Jats. His arms and a leg had to be amputated. The attack was because he dared to file criminal charges against Jat villagers who raped his 17-year-old daughter four years previous.

Kurnool. March 2005: About 1,600 miles south of Delhi, eight Dalits were killed over a land-related dispute.

Shankarbigha. January 1999: About 800 miles east of Delhi, 23 Dalits were killed over a land-related dispute.

Keeripatti, Madurai District, Tamil Nadu. April 2005: V. Ashagumalai resigns as panchayat president (local area leader) within minutes of getting elected. He was a Dalit and the Hindu Thavar community could not imagine being ruled by him, so even those who voted for him wanted him to step down.

Tamil Nadu. December 2005: After the Asian tsunami, Dalit survivors were thrown out of relief camps by non-Dalits who refused to share makeshift homes, common kitchens, toilets, etc.

Tuticorin, Tamil Nadu. June 2004: Non-Dalits ban Dalit owned dogs from entering their part of town. They feared that Dalit dogs might mate with their dogs.

Kaundampatti, Tamil Nadu. September 2004; and Punjab. November 2004: Dalit youth forced to drink his own urine after fighting back against tormentors.

As if the stories already told were not enough, it is also shocking to learn that caste's consequences are not limited to India. Dalits in other parts of the world also face oppression and inequalities. Tom Brake, Liberal Democrat Member of Parliament for Carshalton and Wallington, and Shadow Secretary of State for International Development (England), said in a parliamentary debate, "Even in the UK there is discrimination against the Dalits. I met some Dalits recently, one of whom is a senior person working at a hospital in Ealing. He said that not he but a woman Dalit colleague of his had encountered enormous problems in establishing her authority as a manager, because the people of a higher caste with whom she worked did not recognize that she could possibly manage them. He said that there was even graffiti in the hospital. Simply the word 'caste', to remind her that she had no authority in the caste system."[17]

Human Rights Watch has extensive coverage of the global issue of caste-based discrimination in "Caste Discrimination: A Global Concern", 2001, citing cases of such intolerance in the USA, the UK, Japan, Sri Lanka, Nigeria, the Persian Gulf region, nearly all of Asia, and the Caribbean. The UN has commissioned special investigators to research and document discrimination based on work and descent.18 In addition, "No Escape: Caste Discrimination in the UK," brings additional references from the UK as researched by the Dalit Solidarity Network.

There can be no doubt that caste and its ghastly consequences go even deeper than racism. The oppressor turns into an inhuman monster. The oppressed become sub-human creatures emptied of their humanity and dignity. The lives of modern-day slaves like Premila and Manjula are eternally affected by this caste-based bondage. The caste plot of Indian civilization is a tragedy unlike anything else. Caste dehumanizes everyone: both the oppressors (the elitist upper castes) and the oppressed (the low castes). For the sake of the real people around the world who face this cruel fate, there must be another way.

As the Good Shepherd Church of India leads the Dalit Freedom Movement within India and around the globe, it does not sit idly by while caste ravages the planet. Our belief is that there must be another ideal that guides everything we do. Our programs to fight against caste-based oppression and help the Dalit people through a five-pillared approach: Education, Healthcare, Economic Development, Spiritual Development and Advocacy/Justice activities. When carefully integrated as one, this approach to eradicating caste and creating freedom for Dalit-Bahujans in India and around the world brings holistic transformation and permanent change for those for whom caste becomes torture: Dalit men, women and children like Latha, Manjula, Premila, and hard-working Dalits whose lives were taken all too prematurely.

The eradication of caste begins with education. We believe education to be the most foundational component of the Good Shepherd Church's quest for Dalit freedom. The Good Shepherd School system provides affordable, high-quality, English-based education to 26,000 children in the first 100 of 300 or more schools is the cornerstone from which the rest of our programming is built. As evidenced so clearly in this chapter, generations of Dalit-Bahujan people have been denied an education and deceived into thinking that an education will not meet the daily needs with which they are confronted so dramatically. The Dalit Freedom Movement wants to give a complete primary and secondary education to Dalit-Bahujan children and young people in the English language, thereby preparing them for a bright future of prosperity and personal growth. The result? We aim to draw Dalit-Bahujans out of the centuries-long endurance of inhumane atrocities, oppression and pain.

The Good Shepherd Healthcare Initiative is the second component in this unique vision for change for the Dalit-Bahujan people. Lack of funding and accessibility for even the most basic of immunizations, nutrition education and preventative health measures have riddled the Dalits with preventable disease which have been eradicated in most of the world. The Dalit Freedom Movement's pilot projects use nearly 100 Community Health Workers to bring Community Health programs, medical interventions, regional clinics and medical education to the greater Dalit-Bahujan population. The Good Shepherd Healthcare Initiative's goals includes reduction in infant mortality rates, as well as a significant reduction in community morbidity rates, plus an improvement in general community health. Any improvement in community health will bring not only physical change to society, but will also bring economic change, emotional change, and an overall greater sense of hope for tomorrow's generation of Dalit-Bahujans.

The third area of focus in the Dalit Freedom Movement's Transformed Community model is the Good Shepherd Economic Development work. When taught how to save money in thousands of Self-Help Groups, and how to invest grant money through Small Business Grant Groups and Vocational Training, Dalit women are able to break out of the caste-based and gender-based oppression in which they exist, and bring positive short-term financial change and a sense of long-term economic transformation. Women learn skills like sewing, desktop publishing and creation of handicrafts with which they can earn money to support their destitute family members. Dalit men are taught to drive, while others are mentored in business entrepreneurship, marketing and banking. Some Dalits are even being trained to enter the Business Processing Offices of the major companies in India's 'Shining' cities like Hyderabad, Bangalore, Delhi and Mumbai.

Advocacy efforts round out the Transformed Community model and present the largest opportunity for international partners to lend their expertise and involvement in freeing Dalits from their caste-produced plight. The way forward for the Dalit people of India is to make the issue of caste oppression a global issue garnering global concern in government offices, in the United Nations, and among the influencers in Hollywood, in big business, in universities, and on Capitol Hill and in Parliament. Spreading the heartbreaking stories of atrocities against Dalits breeds awareness that gets people involved. A brighter tomorrow is on the horizon for the Dalit-Bahujans if only more people around the world will join with the Good Shepherd Church and the Dalit Freedom Movement as advocates, as a voice for the voiceless and oppressed.

With the world involved in passionate and committed unity for the betterment of all humanity, caste and its consequences do not stand a chance. The atrocities against Dalits we have now explored in great detail can indeed be eradicated as people from around the world work together for Dalit freedom and the inherent rights and liberties that accompany this movement.

One of the most coveted freedoms for which we are all fighting is explored in the next chapter.

Finding food, clothing and shelter is an everyday problem for Dalits.

Dalit women face unimaginable atrocities. They are considered doubly oppressed — due to both their caste and gender.

Over 3,000 years of caste-based oppression subjects 300 million Dalits — and another 450 million in other marginalized backward castes — to extreme poverty.

Dalits are forced to do the dirtiest and lowliest of jobs, those that the upper castes consider unclean and "beneath them." Danger, injury and low pay only make it worse.

Many young Dalit girls are forced to work long hours every single day for very little pay. Though paid some amount, most consider the work just mere pennies away from forced slavery.

The word "harijans" originally referred to children born to temple prostitutes. Today harijans are unfortunately still a tragic part of Dalit society.

Saving the children — especially the girls, who face the worst oppression — is a priority for the Dalit Freedom Movement.

Dalit women are deemed worthless in caste-based society. Traditionally, they have no legitimate hope of change or improvement. They have resigned themselves to be beaten, abused, worked as servants and dismissed as equal humans.

Dalit women are sold into human trafficking in the sex industry.

Dalit children are sold into bonded labor and work in dangerous conditions.

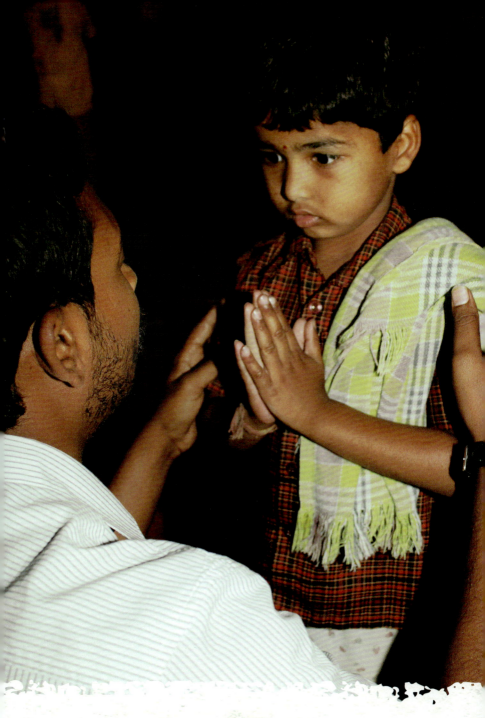

True love rescues children and women from exploitation. True love defends the weak. True love protects those who can't protect themselves. Just as Christ did.

Education is one of the fundamental keys to Dalit freedom. Good Shepherd Schools (Dalit Education Centers) give children an English education in a full academic schedule, as well as teach them self-discipline and instill hope for the future.

Good Shepherd English Medium Schools provide more than 30,000 Dalit children with a critically important education. Without education, Dalits are doomed to repeat their parents' oppression because of ignorance. With education, Dalits can advance to higher education and a worthwhile career.

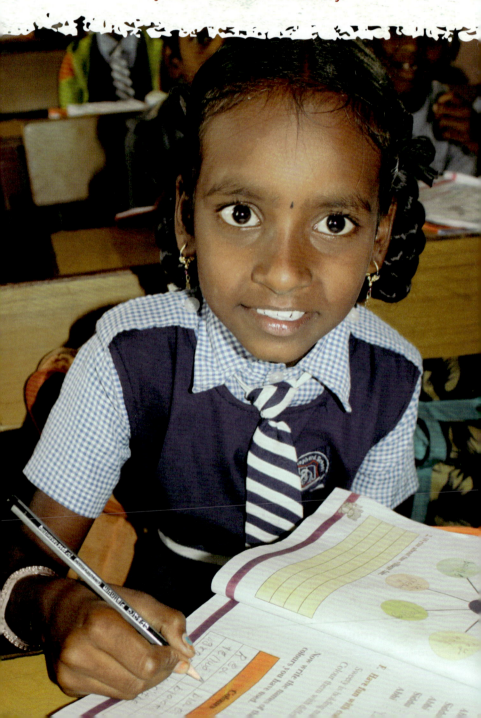

Dalit girls are given an equal opportunity to learn in the Dalit Freedom Movement. For many, it is their only way out of a lifetime of slavery.

Community-based accountability brings success to Good Shepherd Self Help Groups. People begin to depend on each other to repay starter grants, grow their businesses and help others improve as they have.

Success comes as men and women learn a new trade, open a business and then teach their children to do the same. This breaks the cycle of poverty.

Good Shepherd Healthcare Clinics are strategically placed in the neediest areas to help with medical assessments and treatments, health and hygiene education and much more. Mobile clinics go to remote areas where needed most.

Good Shepherd Healthcare Workers provide quality healthcare for every man, woman and child they can. This service is vital to a thriving Dalit community. Healthcare workers are changing the face of Dalit villages across India.

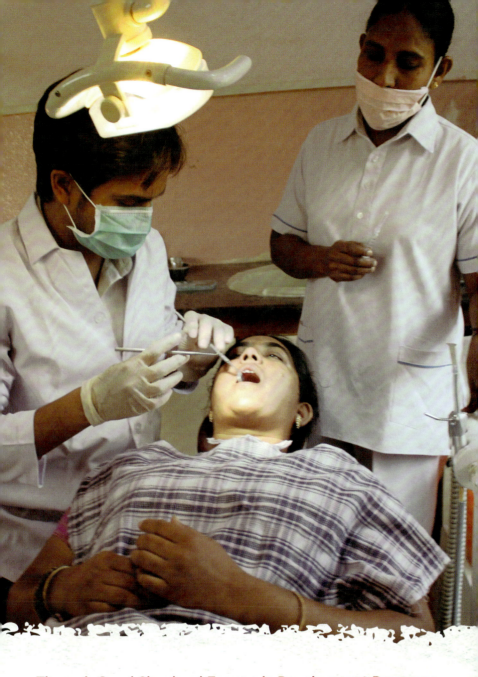

Through Good Shepherd Economic Development Programs, Dalits can be trained to work in the fields of technology, medicine, engineering and law. Dalit women in Good Shepherd Self Help Groups are earning money and learning a vocation. Dalit men are learning the importance of remaining with their families and earning a sufficient income.

Currently there are thousands of Good Shepherd Self Help Groups in Dalit communities where people learn to band together and improve their lives with grants and financial education for new small businesses.

Dalits want to leave behind traditional unskilled work and join the global marketplace through proper education.

Good Shepherd Job Training Centers help Dalit adults develop practical skills which can move them out of poverty and into the modern age.

The Christian Church pledges full solidarity with the Dalits, and the Good Shepherd Church of India leads the way in full support of eradicating caste from all churches.

Dalit Freedom Workers are dedicated to prayer, living a disciplined life and preaching the gospel in word and deed to all people. These Indian national workers give their lives through persecution, financial hardships and many different struggles to show the *Dayasagar*® film, start churches and be pastors. Without their undying efforts, there would be no Dalit freedom.

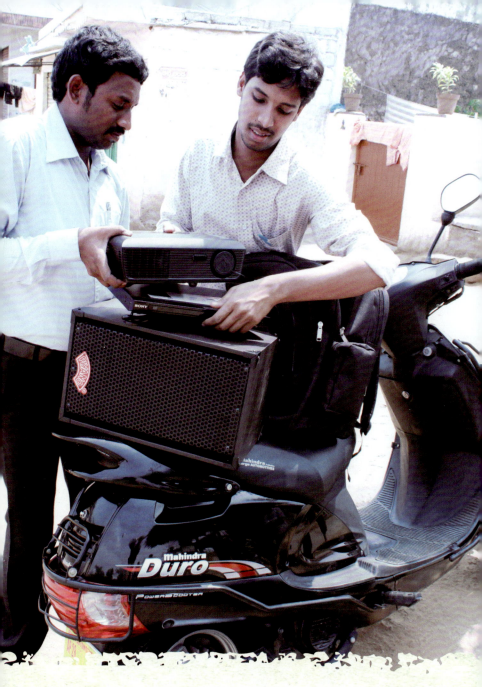

Teams of workers go all over India — traveling mostly by two-wheeled scooters with specially designed equipment to show *Dayasagar*® to villagers in the most remote places as well as the biggest cities. "How beautiful are the feet of those who bring good news!" (Romans 10:15).

Dayasagar®, our all-Indian acted Life of Christ film, is shown all over India night after night. People come to know who Jesus is by watching His birth, death and resurrection. Many for the first time. Churches are started from the seeds *Dayasagar®* plants.

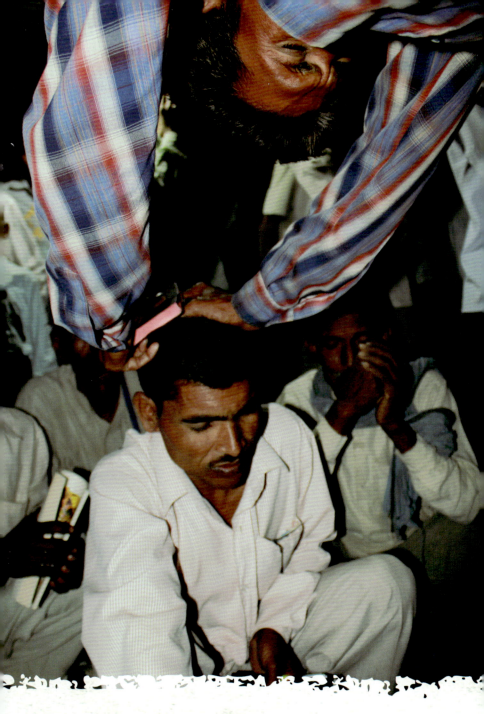

In Jesus' name, Dalit Freedom Workers pray for the sick and counsel the needy. "So if the Son makes you free, you will be free indeed" (John 8:36).

Currently, there are thousands of Good Shepherd Churches. These churches become community centers for the village and surrounding area, as often job training and medical services are based here.

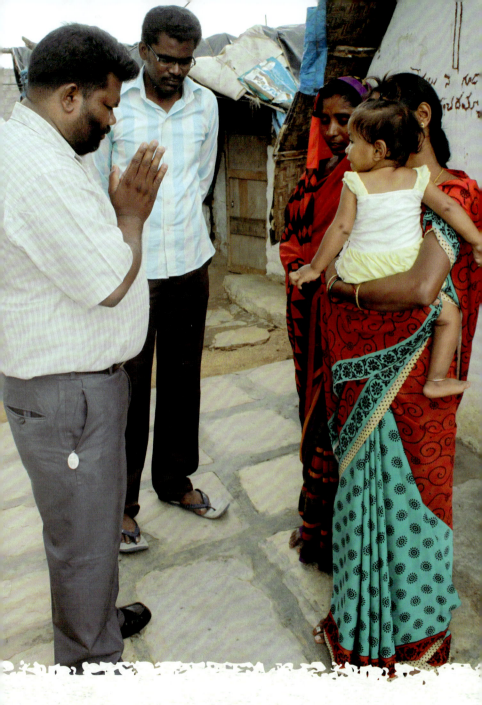

There are thousands of Good Shepherd Home Fellowship Groups that meet regularly. Many of these home fellowships will eventually grow and become new churches where a permanent pastor is assigned.

The church growth movement is really growing because it brings real hope and true, long-lasting transformation. Now whole families are coming to faith in Christ.

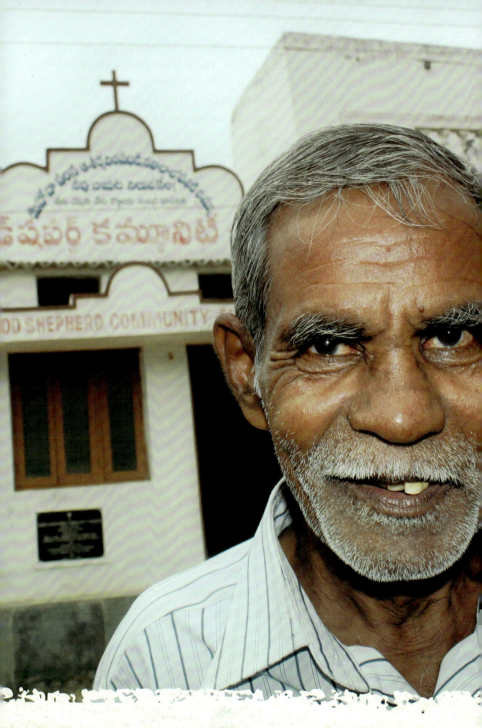

In Jesus, Dalit men learn to take responsibility for their actions, care for their families and train the next generation.

In Jesus, Dalit women become whole in mind, body and spirit. Unshackled, they now know they are loved, that God Almighty values them and that they have true, everlasting freedom.

CHAPTER FOUR

THE MOST VALUABLE FREEDOM

One of the key issues caste-based oppression brings to the forefront of human thought is freedom of conscience. Dalit oppression is a nightmare. As part of this oppression, Dalits are denied another fundamental human right: the freedom of conscience, which is the ability to make individual choices, especially with regard to religious beliefs and moral activity. The denial of this right completes the Dalit hell on earth.

Dalits are permanently bonded to their status as outcastes. There is nothing within Indian society that can transform them into members of the upper castes — not even education, money or position, as Dr. B.R. Ambedkar and others discovered to their deep sadness. Caste does not allow upward mobility. The upper castes' demand for full subservience by the Dalits has only intensified under the growth of the extremist Hindutva movement. For the people we have already met in this book — people like Latha, Manjula, Premila and the family members of those brutally murdered in Haryana and in Orissa — there is absolutely no hope for a better future for them within the realms of the caste system. According to the religiously and socially sanctioned norms of caste, Dalit-Bahujans have no freedom to choose for themselves a belief system that will offer the hope for which they so desperately long.

The laws of caste are detailed in the Manusmriti, a much-despised book written by Manu, a priestly scribe within the Hindu faith. Tens of thousands of copies of this book of codes detailing the caste system have been distributed in the villages and towns of India in the early part of the twenty-first century in an attempt to garner greater modern-day support and steadfast compliance with

Hindutva, the philosophy of right-wing fundamentalist Hinduism which believes that India is for Hindus and should be ruled only by Hindus. The Hindutva forces believe in the inseparability of politics and religion, and that minorities should abide by and live at the mercy or goodwill of the majority. The Hindutva regime would like to establish one race (Hindu), one culture (Hindu) and one religion (Hinduism) in the Indian sub-continent. All other religious groups are considered a minority. Brahmanism dominates Hindutva ideology.

The growth of the Hindutva movement has coincided with a directly proportional increase in the number of atrocities against Dalits. In day-to-day life, upper caste society is desperate to remain separated from the Dalits, lest they suffer socio-spiritual contamination. However, rather than freeing the Dalits from the Hindu caste system as a possible measure of complete religious and ritual purification, upper caste society uses force and allurement to retain the Dalit people in this system that forever considers them outcastes.

Every attempt is made to maintain the power structure of the upper castes. Without the slavery of the caste system, the whole edifice of the upper caste power structure comes apart religiously, socially and economically. Therefore, the upper castes cannot allow freedom of conscience for Dalit-Bahujans or they risk the demolition of the entire mechanism ordaining them with power and catering to their narcissistic long-term goals for society and the nation.

Because of this systematic discrimination on the religious front and in the realm of the conscience, the silent exodus of the Dalits from Brahmanism's social order continues unabated despite violent attempts by the upper castes at its prevention. It is critical to understand that this movement is an exodus of revolt against an evil and sinful structure. Those who are "sinned against" are freely and willingly striking back at their oppressors spiritually and socially. Neither force nor fraudulent means are being employed by Christians or by any of the other faiths currently embraced by Dalits.

Dalits are breaking out of the system that ensnares them and are desperately grasping at their brass ring: the right to choose.

Early in modern India's history, a Presidential ordinance allegedly created "protection" for the Dalits with regard to various aspects of their economic growth and stability.1 However, in actuality, the State became party to wider discrimination against Dalits. Within the parameters of this Order, the State favors those labeling themselves "Hindu" even though Dalits have had no social or spiritual rights within the Hindu caste system for over 3,000 years. For instance, Dalits cannot become priests in a temple or the high priests of the Hindu religion occupying the status of a Shankaracharya (the main acknowledged seat or throne of Hinduism).

The ordinance initially favored the granting of affirmative action privileges only to those Dalits labeled Hindu. Dalits of other faiths had no access to these privileges. Once again the Dalits were obviously targeted and their freedom to choose their faith compromised. Their daily economic and physical survival depends on them clinging to an ideology which denies them the right to be human.

This continued systematic caste-based discrimination, with special regard to the freedom of conscience, is the subject of a heated debate and misunderstanding, both nationally and internationally. An international conference panel member confronted me with an interesting question once in Brussels. "We were told Gandhi ended the caste system in India!" he exclaimed when I finished speaking on the caste issue at an inter-parliamentary conference. Like many others around the world, he believed that caste was no longer a problem. He believed Dalits were merely poor and had the power to choose a better life.

Not surprised by his statement, I responded that when I was going to school in the 1960s and 1970s I was also told that the caste system had ended in India. I was told that the problem of the caste system was eradicated by the Constitution. As an adult I quickly realized that the caste system was alive and active among peoples of South Asia. Subsequently, through a set of personal circumstances, I began to understand the horrors of caste discrimination and the dehumanization unleashed on the Scheduled Castes and Scheduled Tribes of India as a result. Whenever Dalits try to assert their rights as human beings or try to exercise the freedom of conscience, they are quickly rebuffed and exposed to new hardships.

Along with many around the world and within India, I agree that Mahatma Gandhi was indeed a great soul and the founding Father of the modern Indian nation. He was a true apostle of non-violence and a peacemaker of communities. His non-violent struggle for Indian independence was unparalleled in a human history strewn with violent struggles for freedom. Indians are proud of him and rightly so.

Gandhi was of course embarrassed and ashamed of the practice of untouchability. He worked hard to deal with it. Sadly, Gandhi's legacy is marred because he did not adequately address the issue of the abolishment of the caste system itself. Some of Gandhi's writing on the caste system in Indian society does not make for happy reading. Gandhi settled for dealing with only the principle symptom of the caste disease: untouchability. That was a huge mistake. So much so that the very word Gandhi created to give dignity to the Dalits, 'harijan,' is today one of the most derogatory words that can be used for the Dalit-Bahujan people.

To achieve true transformation within the Indian nation, Gandhi should have applied the great Dr. Bhim Rao Babasaheb Ambedkar's agenda of abolishing the system that gave birth to the heinous practice of untouchability in the Indian social order.

Abolishing caste would have ensured freedom of conscience for all.

Today Ambedkar's true contribution to the nation, his work for the depressed castes, is more deeply understood and appreciated. Even the upper caste movements and political leaders began to co-opt Ambedkar's legacy and brand name as their own.

As Ambedkar's views and revolutionary thought came to the forefront of Indian society, the stark differences between the Father of the Nation and the Father of the Constitution were laid bare. Ambedkar's bitter philosophical disagreement with Mahatma Gandhi was no longer locked in archival documents. Gradually, Ambedkar's opposing sentiment became common knowledge: Ambedkar wanted the abolishment of caste itself, which would result in abolishing untouchability and the inhuman discrimination against the Dalits.

Perhaps Gandhi's tragically flawed proposal of dealing only with untouchability was influenced by the orthodox upper caste people who surrounded him, telling him that Hinduism as they knew it would not survive the demise of caste, its foundation, steel frame and bonding force.

But today, more than fifty years after Independence, caste prejudice and discrimination within Brahmanism's worldview continue as a persistent disease. Gandhi's attempts to battle untouchability have gone unrealized. History has proven Ambedkar right. The Indian Constitution should have banned the caste system along with the problem of untouchability. Trying to remove untouchability without removing the caste system was like dealing with mere symptoms rather than combating the root disease. Freedoms of all kinds for all people are only guaranteed when caste is gone. Caste must be annihilated if untouchability is to be genuinely eliminated.

Ambedkar concluded that conversion (the exercise of Dalit freedom of conscience with regard to religious beliefs) was the ultimate solution for the Dalit-Bahujan people if Hinduism was not able to reform itself and annihilate caste. Ambedkar did not see much hope that this cataclysmic reformation of the Hindu ideology would ever take place. Therefore, led by Ambedkar's philosophies, Dalits and Backward Castes have seen an exit to egalitarian faiths as a way out of caste-based bondage. Religious freedom and spiritual rights remain a fundamental component of the Dalit struggle for emancipation.

Consistent with his desire to help Dalits choose a better way, Ambedkar championed religious freedom for the Dalits and led hundreds of thousands of Dalits into Buddhism in 1956 at a public ceremony in Nagpur, Maharashtra, in Central India. Even though an individual Dalit person would have little success in choosing religious freedom and no power to make a difference in their own community, Dalits banning together and participating in a mass movement away from caste oppression into a freedom-based religious belief system are able to gain much-needed ground in this fundamental fight. Ambedkar spearheaded this conversion movement.

In a counter-move, upper caste political leaders devised and passed several anti-conversion laws in the dubious name of "freedom of religion." Christians were falsely accused of forced and fraudulent conversions. These laws have been a deliberate move to keep the Dalits locked in the dehumanizing caste system. Conversion away from the Hindu ideology means the loss of power for the upper castes, therefore demanding fast action on their part to preserve their much beloved and centuries-long way of life. Freedom to choose for the Dalit-Bahujans marks the ultimate doom for the upper castes.

With the modern-day rise and the destructive specter of right-wing Hindu fundamentalism and fascism (which advocates a return to a so-called "Hindu India" where the caste structure dominates and rules), Ambedkar's struggle and thoughts have become hugely relevant, not only for the oppressed sections of India, but also for Indian nationalism itself.

As mentioned earlier, during the national rule of the right-wing Bhartiya Janata Party (BJP) during the 1990s, the extremist right-wing groups distributed huge quantities of the book the "Manusmriti" which codified and imposed the caste system on the Indian masses. In an effort to further spread their fundamentalist views and curtail Ambedkar's conversion movement away from caste, Hindutva followers wanted everyone to read this book written by the lawgiver, Manu, whose statue stands prominently on the premises of the High Court of Rajasthan. Within the pages of this text, it states that if a low caste person hears the word of God, he should have molten lead poured into his ears. Articulating the name of the Lord invites having his tongue cut off. Other infringements of caste laws carry the death penalty. Is it any wonder that the powerful upper castes perpetuate violence against Dalit women, Dalit men, and Dalit children with such impunity? Their own 'law' allows and encourages such treatment. The violence is only increasing and Dalit-Bahujans themselves agree with Ambedkar that the only escape from caste oppression is the embracing of other religious ideologies. This is the movement that carries forward today. Dalits must have the right to choose.

The movement by Dalits to other religions continues in mass conversion events such as the conversions to Islam at Meenakshipuram, Tamil Nadu, nearly 20 years ago; the conversion of an estimated 100,000 Dalits on November 4, 2001, to Buddhism in New Delhi; and the conversion of Dalits to Buddhism and Christianity in Chennai and Nagpur in recent years.

With regard to the conversions to Islam over 20 years ago at Meenakshipuram, a recent news magazine survey reported that there was not a single Dalit out of the 1,000 or so who converted that regretted his decision to leave Brahmanism's social order. They were glad to be rid of the abominable caste identity they had carried for so long. As a result, they were self-confident and assertive. No upper caste person dared to disrespect them by calling them derogatory, slanderous names. Their caste identity is a thing of the past.

A similar response was elicited by a good percentage of those who recently embraced Buddhism or Christianity, despite the major stumbling block of the practice of caste within the Christian community.2 Despite violence, intimidation and Brahmanism's systematic conspiracy to remove every personal freedom, the Dalits continue to press for freedom of conscience, the most basic and most valuable of all freedoms given to mankind.

Standing in solidarity with the Dalit movement to embrace other religious ideologies was for India's Christians the essence and a practical demonstration of the Christian view of freedom of conscience. For Christians, freedom of conscience is based on their view of creation, mankind and the free will given to humanity. If Christians really believe in religious liberty and freedom of conscience, then we must give genuine freedom to everyone to choose their own faith or to choose no faith at all.

In the mass conversion event in November 2001, the Dalit people, along with one of their main present-day national leaders, Dr. Udit Raj, asserted the right to choose a faith they believed would deliver them from the clutches of the Hindu caste system. While the apparatus of the State was deployed to prevent these people bonded for 3,000 years to exercise their right of conscience, Christians boldly stood in support of them.

We dared to defy the State's infringing upon the personal conscience of the Dalit people.

As Christians, our love for the Dalit people is like the love of Christ for them: unconditional. It is not dependent upon them coming to faith in Christ. We love people whether or not they choose to follow Jesus. The Hindutva lie is that Christian love always has an ulterior motive: conversion to Christianity. This is simply not true.

We love the Dalit-Bahujan people unreservedly. True Christian love is the agape kind of love — genuine, free and everlasting. We are able therefore to hold an unwavering faith in the life and teachings of Christ and love all people completely, even our enemies. This love for them longs for their freedom to exercise their God-given free will with regard to all aspects of life.

As we will discuss more in Chapter Eight, despite the overarching call to unconditional Christ-like love, the Christian Church has not always been open to the Dalit plight. Even today, fostering this attitude of unconditional love and solidarity with the Dalit-Bahujan people as they embrace their freedom of conscience, especially with regard to religious choice, is a difficult issue for some to comprehend.

Therefore, an important part of the Dalit Freedom Movement's international campaign is to educate worldwide partners and others interested in the Dalit-Bahujan movement on the importance of accepting the Dalit people into the Christian fold, even as they are looking for other religious ideologies that might welcome them wholeheartedly.

Sadly, this is easier said than done in some cases. Some local Christian leaders have not displayed the same 'open door' to Dalit-Bahujans as have Buddhists and Muslims. In fact, these leaders are on record saying it would be better for "somebody else" to take care of these new converts to Christianity as they cannot handle the police harassment and intimidation. This is going to be a recurring problem wherever churches seek to protect their institutions or where they do not understand the nature of the Dalit movement to the Christian faith.

A deep-seated revolt against an evil socio-religious system drives the Dalit movement, both as individuals and as communities. Another problem that prevents Christians from embracing the Dalit movement is that some Christians cannot relate to this deep-seated inner rebellion. They do not understand that it is the rebellion against being treated as less worthy than animals, as people who are not made in the image of God. It is the rebellion against the denial of any spiritual right, the denial of the right to priesthood and the denial of full salvation in this life. It is the rebellion against complete dehumanization and pathetic social and economic conditions.

Is it not possible that the movement toward a Christian ideology that comes through this kind of rebellion and sees people turn their back on a socio-spiritual way of life is more sincere than the nominal conversions that take place in Christian communities and nations? The rebellion of the Dalits a powerful "turning away from" that which has brought them both social and spiritual death. Is this not a colossal change of mind?

Whatever the case, the Global and Indian Church carries an enormous responsibility now. The Dalits are in exodus. What will be the story two decades from now when some section of the media studies the masses of Dalits who have turned to Christ? Will they say that they found the equality and dignity of Christ within the Indian Church? Will their predominant identity be that they are Christians? Or will they still be Syrians, Nadars, Dalits, or some other caste?

For millennia, the upper castes taught the Dalits that they were born as untouchables because of their sinful past life. This teaching goes beyond the doctrine of original sin. Not only are they sinners in the present life, but they have been sinners in the past life. This is the doctrine of pre-birth original sin. Will the Dalits two decades from now have fully accepted the forgiveness of sin that Christ offers at the Cross so that they know deliverance from the notion that God is punishing them and does not love them? Will they experience the liberation of being counted as sons and daughters of God? Will they exult in their adoption as the children of God?

It depends upon how the Indian Church responds to this new challenge. We will expand on this discussion in Chapter Eight. For now, however, we pray that the Dalits' most valuable freedom, the freedom of conscience, will be activated within Dalit-Bahujan society, and that as they convert en masse to other religious ideologies, that religious leaders across the nation and around the world will open their arms in warm acceptance of this people who are longing for eternal escape.

We move on now to examine those who have chosen Buddha as their answer to the problem of caste.

CHAPTER FIVE

BUDDHA OR JESUS: A DALIT DILEMMA

So far in our journey we have investigated the plight of the Dalit people. We have witnessed the dire consequences the caste system produces for the forgotten and the oppressed. We have learned that true freedom begins with the freedom to choose, the freedom to exercise personal, God-given free will. It is this freedom to choose that we now further explore. When Dalits come together en masse to break free from the bondage of caste, what will they choose? What is their best option?

The Dalit exodus toward Islam, Buddhism and Christianity in the state of Haryana, where the lynching of the five Dalits took place, stunned the nation. It was October 27, 2002, just 12 days after the murder of their fellow Dalits. Udit Raj, the Dalit leader who led the Dalits in embracing Buddhism in 2001, organized a symbolic conversion event for local Dalits who were outraged with the killing of the five young men. On a crowded street corner in the center of town, several hundred Dalit leaders gathered in open revolt. Bollywood film director Mahesh Bhatt (a noted human rights activist), leaders of the Muslim community, and leaders of the All India Christian Council (aicc) were present at this revolutionary meeting.

The first Dalit to convert to Islam on that day decided to take "Saddam Hussein" as his new name to demonstrate his rebellion against the caste system. Others became Buddhists as Udit Raj had done earlier.

At the rally, Mr. and Mrs. Chandra Bhan, two bank officers,

both Dalits, chose to embrace Christianity. It was their personal choice. They were not forced or coerced into choosing Christ, but rather they were absolutely convinced when they expressed their decision to change their religious identity. There was no ambiguity about what they were doing because they had done their research. Theirs was a carefully considered, final decision. In no uncertain terms they declared they would be following Jesus.

This decision by the Bhan family was not an easy one. They knew there would be consequences. However, they were willing to pay the heavy price for leaving their socio-spiritual system and turning to the Christian faith. They believed that in Christianity they would find the dignity and the freedom from caste-based oppression they sought. Though the police harassed this couple, they remained steadfast in their decision. In all reality, the wife could lose her job and their children may lose the affirmative action benefits they now enjoy. Still, this strong-willed family has not wavered in the midst of tremendous pressure and threat.

Dalits like the Bhan family are becoming more willing to endure pressure and threat to find freedom. They take their inspiration from possibly the most highly respected Dalit leader of all time, Dr. B.R. Ambedkar.

As we learned in the last chapter, Ambedkar spearheaded the first major socio-spiritual movement of the Dalit people in 1956. He asked them to move away from Hinduism.[1] He was an educated leader who received a doctorate in law in the United States. However, despite his credentials, upon his return to India he found that his social and religious status had not changed in the opinion of caste-minded Hindus. He continued to face caste-based discrimination.

Disgusted by this ill-treatment, Ambedkar led a non-violent revolt against the caste system. He used his influence to ensure that the new Indian Constitution would ban the practice of untouchability. In fact, he tried to banish it completely. Article 17 of the Constitution reads, "Untouchability is abolished and its practice in any form is forbidden. The enforcement of any disability arising out of untouchability shall be an offense punishable in accordance with law." In keeping with this provision, in 1955, the Indian Parliament passed "The Untouchability Offenses Act", which sadly, although well-intentioned, was not widely adopted into the everyday practice of society and required further development and implementation in later decades. The US State Department International Religious Freedom Report 20062 notes "The Scheduled Castes and Scheduled Tribes (Prevention of Atrocities) Act of 1989 lists offenses against disadvantaged persons and provides for stiff penalties for offenders; however, this act has had only a modest effect in curbing abuse due to victims' fears of retaliation if they accused high-caste members of committing atrocities. Inter-caste violence was especially pronounced in Uttar Pradesh, Bihar, Rajasthan, Madhya Pradesh, Tamil Nadu, and Andhra Pradesh, and reportedly claimed hundreds of lives. Human rights NGOs alleged that caste violence, which crossed religious lines, remained at prior years' levels."

Though the Indian Constitution banned the practice of untouchability, the caste system itself was not abolished. The law merely addressed one major symptom of the more serious problem of a caste ideology. Today, the penalties apportioned for caste-based discrimination are rarely implemented because those responsible for law enforcement are often the upper castes who are themselves biased by caste.

Ambedkar's disillusionment with the inability of the law to deal with the practice of untouchability and its reinforcement of the caste system forced him to look for other religious systems offering the Dalits an escape. At one point he threatened to burn the very Constitution framed under his chairmanship.

His search for another religious way of life began early in his life. He declared that though he was born a Hindu, he would not die a Hindu. His search for an alternative led him to a new version of Buddhism derived from his studies on the birth and growth of Buddhism in India.

During his search, Ambedkar investigated Christianity.

Although he saw a host of good, equality-laden attributes within the Christian faith, he also saw clear drawbacks in the Indian Christian Church and in the lives of Christians of his day. Because of this, he considered Christianity not viable for the Dalit people. India was under British rule and the Christianity at that time was closely associated with colonialism.

Ambedkar recognized the fact that Jesus stood out against the caste system. However, he also saw that Indian Christianity had been poisoned by caste-based oppression. He could not accept the fragmented Church which was riddled with its own form of caste-based politics. Ambedkar wanted a religion that would unite his people and bring cohesion to the thousands of sub-castes. He wanted a faith that was willing to work at the core of society and not at its margins; a faith that was not artificially divided into the "spiritual" and the "non-spiritual." He sought a belief system that affected all areas of Dalit life.

Eventually, Ambedkar chose Buddhism because of its casteless society and unilateral equality. Buddhism as an ideology rejected the caste system. Buddhism rejected idolatry, the idea of reincarnation, and the possibility that Buddha, himself, was an incarnation of God. Buddhism also gave equality to women.

Despite the success of Ambedkar's embracing of Buddhism, the conversion event he sponsored (Maharashtra, 1956) did not become the greatly anticipated mass exodus out of the Hindu caste system because of the lack of an empowered Dalit leadership during Ambedkar's era. Dalit assertion would take at least another four decades before it would become a major socio-religious force in India. Ambedkar was the visionary. However, he needed the backing and reinforcement of other national-level leaders, as well as grass-roots movements in both the urban and rural areas.

The present-day Dalit Freedom Movement in India has both the visionaries, like Udit Raj, and the reinforcements. On the national, regional, state and village level, there are enthusiastic leaders among the Dalit community who will fight to make the Dalit agenda known and who will motivate the masses to take part in the hoped for radical transformation of communities. Today, no political party in India can ignore the well-organized Dalit movement as it gains momentum.

The success of the Dalit movement in the modern-day era gives Dalits a choice. Will Buddhism remain the number one choice for fulfilling all the felt needs of the Dalit-Bahujan people? Or will Christianity and/or Islam emerge as the clear choice as Dalits move onward and upward, battling caste-based oppression?

Ambedkar started it all, but was forced to leave the results to future generations. It is now to his legacy and the practical outcomes of his philosophy and efforts that we turn. What does Dalit leadership look like today? It is time to meet two men — one who lived before Ambedkar and one who lives after — whose life and work attributed to making Ambedkar's unrealized dreams come true: Periyar and Udit Raj.

CHAPTER SIX

AMBEDKAR: THE MOSES OF THE DALITS

Though Ambedkar's conversion movement did not encompass all Dalits nationwide and did not provide the passionately desired, immediate end to the caste system, the ideology surrounding his Dalit quest for freedom has gained strength. Ambedkar's dream for the full freedom of the Dalit people did not happen during his lifetime; he was not able to enter the hallowed 'promised land' of Dalit emancipation. However, today Ambedkar's influence continues to grow in dominance in Indian society. India's current major caste upheaval can be attributed directly to his work and writings.

Today's Dalit leadership is strong, motivated and equipped to continue Ambedkar's mission. The strength of the modern day movement can be attributed in part to the contribution of two passionate and committed men. First we turn to a man who lived in the early twentieth century whose work still makes a remarkable difference among Dalit-Bahujans today: Periyar.

Over the years, leaders for the liberation of the Dalits have thrived in states like Tamil Nadu and other places along the southern tip of India where caste discrimination has been particularly strong. E.V. Ramasamy, known to the masses as Periyar, is perhaps the most famous from this region. ('Periyar' means 'respected one' or 'an elder' in the Tamil language. His name has also been transliterated as 'Ramaswami.')

Periyar lived from 1879 to 1973. A powerful communicator, he wrote prolifically in the Tamil language and gave speeches almost 250 days a year during his prime. One speech could change the habits and practices of a village forever. According to one sociologist, "His speeches, which were earthy and peppered with parables, proverbs and local language use, were tremendously popular, in part precisely because they never obeyed the rules and conventions of accepted middle-class public address."[1]

An ardent atheist and rationalist, Periyar believed religion and superstition were an evil. After a speech in the village of Poonthottam in 1944, the entire village gave up Hinduism and embraced atheism. The local temple was leveled, the idol dumped into the pond, and Brahmin priests banned from certifying marriages or performing death rituals. Even today the village continues these practices.[2]

Not surprisingly, Periyar faced opposition from the government. He and his sister were arrested on charges of sedition in 1933. He also faced routine harassment from nationals; his enemies would attack him during speeches by throwing sandals, stones, cow dung, human excreta, or eggs.[3] He did not mince words when speaking of his hatred of the caste system, untouchability and Brahmanism. His brilliant oratorical and philosophical debating skills, a natural gift considering he quit school after fourth grade, led some to call him the "Socrates of Southeast Asia."[4]

As a young man, he took a pilgrimage to Varanasi, a holy city to Hindus due its location on the Ganges River. There he witnessed serious discrimination against non-Brahmins that changed him forever. While he later became a successful businessman, he remained a committed social activist, politician and reformer.[5]

Periyar's life, work and obvious boldness and passion for the Dalit cause make him a major figure in the historical Dalit quest for emancipation. He played on the same team as Ambedkar. He was a mentor to modern-day activists. One such activist, the twenty-first century's brightest figure in the Dalit Freedom Movement, is Dr. Udit Raj. It is to his story that we turn as we see Ambedkar's objectives for freedom, equality and human rights for the Dalit people become a reality.

⤙ ✳ ⤚

Dr. Udit Raj is one of today's prominent Dalit leaders. He is the Chairman of the All India Confederation of Scheduled Castes/Scheduled Tribes Associations, an advocacy organization including government employees, unions and federations. He was born to Dalit parents who were denied a decent life. His given name was Ram Raj. The Week, a well-known magazine in India, describes his family conditions best. "Raj hails from a humble family. 'My parents were poor peasants and I had to face tremendous discrimination. We were treated like dirt,' says Raj. He adds that he 'always wanted to dedicate his life to the people'."[6] It was this desire to help his people that drove Ram Raj to make the most of every opportunity he was given as a young person to improve his life and the life of his family.

As young Ram Raj grew and made great sacrifices to get an education, he discovered the equality due him as a citizen of India. He took advantage of the available affirmative action provisions for him and found a job as an officer in the Indian Revenue Service (IRS), a government agency.

Ram Raj's passion for his people caused tremendous controversy because of his job and because of his passion to bring Dalit rights to the attention of Indian society and the world. However, he knew that he and his compatriots must take a radical stand for their rights as the oppression of the Dalit people continued relentlessly. Casteism locked the Dalits into a life plagued by tyranny of the upper castes.

Through the years since Ambedkar, Dalits have been embracing other faiths en masse, but in uncoordinated events across individual states of the nation. With a vision to encourage the maximum number of his fellow Dalits to leave the caste system, in 2001 Ram Raj and his organization gave thought to lead Dalits everywhere to find freedom and liberty in other religious systems providing personal dignity and spiritual development. The caste system could not offer this to the Dalit people.

On November 4, 2001, the day arrived for this pan-Indian attempt at breaking free from caste-based slavery. Several thousand Dalits who had arrived the night before slept in the open air in New Delhi, the capital city of India. They had traveled by bus, by train, and even on foot. Others streamed in throughout the next day from Punjab, Rajasthan, Bihar and Maharashtra. They were making their way to the capital to publicly disown the religion that had for so long rejected them. Most did not know what to expect, but they made the trek anyway, longing for any chance at freedom. They could no longer endure the oppression that had plagued them. They could no longer bear to be the untouchables, the unseeables[7] and the unapproachables[8] of Indian society. This day would be their chance to change. This day would be the beginning of social, political and spiritual transformation.

Authorities tried to discourage the Dalit gathering. Approximately 24 hours prior to the event, the police revoked the permission organizers had obtained to conduct the event at the Ram Lila Grounds, a large, popular venue in the heart of New Delhi. Simultaneously, hundreds of thousands of Dalits making their way to the capital were stopped by police and other opponents at state borders. Additionally, some newspapers and posters falsely announced the rally had been cancelled. Threats of violence against Dalits multiplied.

Initially disheartened but not deterred, organizers of the event found an alternate location for the event, which ironically also had a sentimental connection. The new location was Ambedkar Bhavan, a special meeting grounds dedicated to the original savior of the Dalits, Dr. B.R. Ambedkar.

By mid-morning on November 4, 2001, the event was underway and tens of thousands of Dalits and interested spectators packed into Ambedkar Bhavan, ready and waiting for the day of transformation to begin. They were seated on the ground, in open windows, on fences and on rooftops. Domestic and international news crews clamored for the best view of this historic ceremony.

"Today this land has taken a bold step! Today we are reborn," declared Raj, who allowed his head to be shaved as part of the "Diksha" (initiation) ceremony. Ram Raj also led the way in changing his first name, "Ram," which was associated with a Hindu god, to "Udit," meaning "arisen." Together with the Buddhist monks who had come to lead these new followers, thousands in the crowd enthusiastically recited the 22 vows of Buddhism. They lifted their hands indicating their allegiance to their new religion, a religion they were choosing without coercion. It was a religion promising them a sense of personal freedom and equality in return.

The Dalits were not alone in their quest for freedom; others actively supported their decision. Representatives of a number of faiths attended the rally in order to express solidarity with the oppressed people's cry for dignity and equality. Three prominent Indian Christian leaders were asked to speak at the rally. One told the crowd of Dalits, "The whole Church of India is with you. We commend you, we are your friends ... The reason we are here is that Jesus Christ also loves you. He died for you. And we promise that the Church of India will bring you the love of Jesus."

This message of the love of God was one the Dalit community had never before heard. Frankly, it was one they had difficulty accepting as true, because they had been brainwashed for centuries into thinking that God could not possibly love them. But that day, the Christian leaders assured the Dalit community of the Eternal's unconditional love for them. This perfect love of the Almighty was the thing that could bring perfect freedom.

In an interview following the Dalit freedom ceremony, I had the privilege to testify to the media. "What happened was incredible: a frontal assault on the caste system and on those who crush Dalit rights. This is a human rights issue. It is our moral duty to stand by the Dalits. If the Church says only one thing, that Jesus Christ loves them, it is the message the Dalit community most needs to hear. They have been told for 3,000 years that God does not love them!"

Other non-Christian participants at the rally agreed with the

Christian standpoint of solidarity and cooperation with the Dalits. Dr. Kancha Ilaiah of Osmania University, Hyderabad, Andhra Pradesh, stated in support of the Christian standpoint, "Why not? What is wrong if [Christians] are helping the masses to be spiritually liberated?"

Following Ambedkar's movement into Buddhism in 1956, the Dalit Freedom Ceremony on November 4, 2001, was a second major, nationally coordinated milestone for the Dalits. In theory and in principle, the day was a success and stands as a pillar of significance for modern-day Dalits. The true question of the event's effectiveness will be answered in time as Dalits across the nation apply the principles embraced on that day in their everyday lives. Will the upper castes stand up and take notice of this revolution for full-life transformation in the lives of more than 250 million people? Will Ambedkar's dream finally be realized? Time will provide the answer, but unlike in 1956 when the Dalit movement was in its infancy, this time the Dalits have the support of all sane, secular and non-partisan Indians. There are still obstacles and opponents determined to obliterate the hopes of Dalits everywhere, but despite these deterrents, for the first time in history, success and freedom appear to be on the horizon.

CHAPTER SEVEN

THE ANTI-CONVERSION CONSPIRACY

Those opposed to Dalit freedom have launched a conspiracy campaign falsely accusing religious leaders of forcibly converting the Dalits. This slanderous accusation is a strategy to put the Christian Church on the defensive for extending a spiritual helping hand to the Dalits and the Other Backward Castes (OBCs). This has resulted in the casteist forces, supported by their militant arms (i.e., Bajrang Dal, Vishwa Hindu Parishad, Hindu Jagran Manch and others) instilling violent fear into the heart and mind of the Indian Church. They want the Church to shut its doors to the oppressed millions who seek holistic liberation and salvation.

This false accusation is primarily intended to demoralize the Christian community, and it has wreaked havoc despite the opponents' failure to produce evidence of cases of forced or fraudulent conversion. The game plan, reminiscent of Nazi propaganda, hinges on repeatedly stating falsehoods until the public believes there must be something suspicious going on about which they do not know.

The lack of evidence of forced conversions to Christianity or any other religion is considerable. The Indian media, in an effort to be fair to both sides of the caste issue, has searched extensively for something that will substantiate the claims of the casteist forces. However, when they check for illegal conversions, they can never find any.

The anti-conversion law in the state of Gujarat was passed in 2003. It officially went into effect on a practical level on April 1,

2008, after the reigning government officials passed "rules" which detailed how police should treat those who violate the law. In the Indian Express News Service, July 12, 2008, we read: "…to a query by Ahmedabad-based Samson Christian of the All India Christian Council [when he sought] to know the number of complaints of forceful conversions made to the police in Gujarat in the last five years, the Home department replied 'only three' — with two of them in 2007. Of the three cases, two were connected with conversion to Christianity in Dahod district, while one, closed by the police for want of evidence, was conversion to Islam in Godhra."

When the brutal attacks against Christians began under the reign of the BJP-led government in 1996, the leaders of the Hindutva brigade raised the bogey of "conversions." Although this was not a new agenda, Christian leaders across the nation were caught unaware both by the viciousness of the attacks by the RSS, the VHP and the Bajrang Dal, and by the tacit political support of these attacks by the ruling BJP government.

After the carnage faced by the churches in the Dangs area of Gujarat in 1998, the BJP Prime Minister called for a national debate on conversion, insinuating in his challenge that Christian conversions were reason enough for the burning of churches. The painful timing of the Prime Minister's utterances again caught the Christians by surprise. Christian leaders argued truthfully that Christian workers were not involved in forced and fraudulent conversions. The civil media heard the statements of the Christians and some papers castigated the Prime Minister for justifying the violence.

In retrospect, I think we should have challenged the Prime Minister directly, not only for a national debate on conversion, but also in creating a further global debate on Dalit and Backward Caste conversions in India. The Christian Church should have set up the meeting in New Delhi in full view of the national and international media. On one side would have been the Prime Minister and the Sangh Parivar. On the other side would be the followers of Ambedkar, Periyar, Phule, and other stalwarts of the Dalit-Bahujan freedom movement. There are enough scholars and spokespersons within the Dalit-Bahujan community to powerfully confront the upper caste-led Sangh Parivar. Dr. Udit Raj, Professor Kancha Ilaiah, Mudra Rakshas (noted Hindi-language scholar and Dalit champion from Uttar Pradesh, North India) and a host of other leaders could have debated the Parivar and its hate propagandists.

When we really look at it, the persecution of Christians has never been about Christians actively engaging in any kind of fraudulent conversions. Rather, Indian Christians oppose the idea of forced conversions and allurement because it is opposed to the spirit of Christ. Typically, the persecution of Christians in India has been about the compassionate reception Christians are commanded to give to all those who are oppressed, victimized, violated and dehumanized. Christians are persecuted because the Sangh Parivar knows that Christ's message of acceptance, love, affirmation, equality, salvation and transformation is the antithesis to the teachings of the caste system.

The Hindutva brigade believes that by using physical force, hate propaganda, institutional harassment, and by passing laws that violate the fundamental rights of human beings, Indian Christians can be intimidated to practice their Christian faith and love only within the confines of their churches.

Instead, the opposite has happened. Despite past rejection of Dalits, modern-day Christian churches have thrown the door wide open to all those who want to enter. Christians have begun more and more to live out Jesus' teachings in word and in deed.

Despite their failure and ineffectiveness in terrorizing Indian Christians and accomplishing their agenda of hate and discrimination, the attacks against Christians still continue unabated today. The Hindutva forces claim they will not cease until they stop Christian compassionate involvement among the Dalits and oppressed peoples. They say they will fight until Christians quit helping Dalits liberate from an oppressed, untouchable life. The power brokers in Indian society want to maintain the social stagnation in India. The power brokers know that an empowered Dalit-Bahujan population will end the 3,000-year rule of minority upper caste forces over a majority population, and they will be out of a job.

The interesting irony in the battle for Dalit emancipation is that the upper caste fraternity has no qualms about their own children being empowered through access to Christian education and Christian charity. For instance, the upper castes flock to Christian educational institutions in the country. Some of the best schools in India are Christian schools founded decades ago on the premise of extending God's love to the masses. The upper caste leadership in the nation is quick to take advantage of this high quality, Christian, English-based education, ensuring their future generations will be equipped to be the power brokers in a free India.

Those accused of fraudulent conversions must then ask: How many upper caste children have been forcibly converted while studying in Christian schools? The answer? None. Yet, this is the accusation they make when Christians get involved in educating Dalit and OBC children.

As a consequence of the ruling castes' double standard, several new anti-conversion bills were enacted. Laws have been passed in Gujarat, Rajasthan, Madhya Pradesh, Chhattisgarh, Arunchal Pradesh, Tamil Nadu, Orissa and Himachel Pradesh.[3]

Of the eight anti-conversion bills passed into law, probably the most controversial was passed in the South Indian state of Tamil Nadu where the per capita Christian population is one of the highest in the nation. Those passing the bill in December 2002 claimed the bill was meant to prevent forced and fraudulent conversions. However, the truth was that the Dalits were willingly and freely embracing other faiths and were facing all the resulting hardships and atrocities.

What the State Government did not anticipate, however, was the response to this unjust law. Everyone quickly realized that the law itself was not against forced or fraudulent conversions. It was a law against Dalits who sought conversion as a way out of the caste prison.

This truth was poignantly demonstrated by the brute force employed by the Tamil Nadu State Government to prevent the Dalit protest on December 6, 2002, during which hundreds embraced Christianity and other faiths. The State had not expected Dalits to stand against the sinister designs of the law. But Dalits knew that this anti-conversion law was meant to forever enslave them in the caste system. They were determined to fight the law and liberate themselves. Despite the law prohibiting them, Dalits in Chennai that day in 2002 embraced Christianity and other faiths.

In a shocking turn of events, the reigning State Government in Tamil Nadu lost the 2004 elections. Soon after the election results were announced, the Tamil Nadu anti-conversion law was repealed. The question remains: What happened to the issue of forced and fraudulent conversions? It became immediately obvious to everyone that the Tamil Nadu anti-conversion law had been politically motivated and designed to enslave and intimidate the Dalits who were willingly exiting the caste system into religious faiths offering them freedom and dignity. The repeal of this law was a small, yet significant victory in the battle for Dalit freedom.

Since 2001, in addition to the anti-conversion laws challenging Dalit and minority socio-political freedom, I have watched with huge embarrassment the upper caste-led English media in India react to the proposal of India's Union Ministry for Human Resources to give the Other Backward Castes reservation (affirmative action rights) in the Central Government-aided institutions of higher learning such as the Indian Institutes of Technology, the Indian Institutes of Management and other central universities.

Although a controversial topic, I believe that for present-day India, this system of reserving guaranteed seats in education, government, and the employment sector is a necessary means to the ends for which we are striving. I provide for you here excerpts from a Times of India newspaper article on the topic of reservation and affirmative action and the present debate as it relates to educational institutions.[4]

"The Supreme Court has done a balancing act on the proposal to have quotas for students from other backward classes in educational institutes run by the central government. The court upheld the proposal but asked for the creamy layer among OBCs to be excluded from the purview of quotas. The ruling should settle the debate on the issue at least for now, but it is time to ask if caste should continue to be the sole criterion to judge social and educational backwardness.

"Caste continues to be an influential social institution. However, the structure of society and the economy is changing, and so too is the influence of caste. Other factors that contribute to social and educational backwardness are coming to the fore. It is time that public policy took note of these changes. These columns have advocated a broad-based deprivation index to replace caste as the sole criterion for measuring backwardness. The reservation policy ought to facilitate affirmative action programmes that focus more on creating equal opportunities than on equal outcomes. In the past, caste was the single most influential factor that dictated whether a person belonged to the socially and educationally advanced classes. The situation is now far more complex. Hence the need for an index of backwardness that takes into consideration not only caste, but also gender, economic conditions and other related factors. The concept of creamy layer recognises that economic factors have to be taken into account while assessing social and educational backwardness.

"The Supreme Court has also said that quotas should not be in perpetuity. That may appear easier said than done considering the centrality of quotas in today's politics. Quotas have become necessary because the reservation policy strives for equal outcomes. The caste system is essentially based on a hierarchy of occupations. Some occupations were privileged over the rest. Social prestige and political power were closely linked to the hierarchy of occupations. India's affirmative action programme had to address this issue. However, there have been major structural changes in the Indian economy. Thanks to technological innovations, new occupations have come up and a few old ones have disappeared. Old social hierarchies based on occupation are increasingly becoming irrelevant. Public policy ought to recognise these changes.

"Quotas are in demand also because there is a shortage of good educational institutions and jobs. Supply-side solutions—more IITs, IIMs and central universities as well as jobs — could ensure that there are no losers. The shrillness of the debate has prevented sensible stocktaking of our affirmative action programmes. It's time to move forward."

This brief excerpt highlights just a few issues and debates going on with regard to this reservation system. Those opposed to the emancipation of the Dalits are also violently opposed to the reservation system. As stated, while reservation benefits are definitely a necessary step on the journey toward the elimination of caste, it is not the end in itself. Caste-based discrimination exists even within the realms of the government-run reservation system.

I am reminded of a story I watched unfold in the excellent documentary, "India Untouched" by Stalin K., who spent four years traveling across India, witnessing and recording firsthand accounts of caste-based discrimination. Stalin tells the story of a university-age Dalit woman who was attending Jawaharalal Nehru Technical University (JNTU) in a 'reserved'/affirmative-action-granted seat. She told story after story of how despite the fact that her academic work matched her classmates, her social activities included attending the same parties and clubs, and her clothing, language and outlook on life were an exact replica of the higher caste students around her, she still bore the pain of caste-based discrimination inflicted by professors and some of her upper caste classmates.

This same girl narrated the account of her Dalit roommate, who had a romantic relationship with an upper caste young man. He had repeatedly confessed his love to this young Dalit woman and spent endless hours with her both in public and in private. However, when the topic of marriage came up, he blatantly refused to continue the relationship, stating caste bias as his reason. When called on to make the intermingling between castes official, discrimination reared its ugly head, even in modern-day India, among modern-day students, in one of the best and most globalized universities in the nation.

I am deeply ashamed at the blindness of educated, secular upper caste India which seems to be completely out of touch with the realities of the social injustices and inequities meted out to the majority Dalit-Bahujan people by the oppressive caste system. Above all there seems to be a complete lack of awareness and understanding of the history of modern India vis-à-vis the caste system, and a total ignorance of the works of Ambedkar, Periyar and Phule. It seems upper caste India wants to be socially ignorant, comfortable, secure and content in their modern, globalized, English-speaking enclave and let the rest of the caste-oppressed Indians be quietly condemned in their own struggle for existence.

One Indian talk show host in 2007 described his television studio audience as a representative sample of "middle class Indians." But when pushed into showing the identity of those English-speaking Indians in the studio, it was clear to those of us who were watching the show across the nation that the studio audience was 90% upper caste.

In another show, the OBC/Dalit minority in the studio staged a walk out because of the farce of the so-called "impartial middle class" India in the studio and the agenda of the show itself, which heavily favored the upper caste audience members.

What is English-speaking, middle class India if not a mainly upper caste India there because of the opportunity, economics, power and freedom enjoyed by upper caste Indians for 3,000 years? The truth is that upper caste India has enjoyed a perverse system of reservation for centuries through the enforcement of the caste system. The minority upper castes comprising just 17% of the population have usurped over 90% of all economic, educational, political, spiritual and social power in India for 3,000 years. Why not discuss that issue in today's media? Is it threatening to the very system that runs India? It is only now in a democratic India that some attempt is being made to redress this horrendous injustice.

Talk of meritocracy in this context is highly hypocritical. Meritocracy works where there has been a consistent level playing field for all over a consistent period. Do most of the Dalits and OBCs have the same level playing field and wealth of opportunities? The truth is that many Dalits and OBCs in the past 50 years have not had access to a highly expensive private English-medium school education, thereby putting them at a distinct disadvantage.5

Why is upper caste India not bearing its shame for what they have done to the oppressed castes in India down through the centuries? Without this sharing of guilt and shame there will be no healing and reconciliation in India. The caste system will bitterly divide and bleed our India.

Why is upper caste India so blind? It seems they walk the streets of India and fail to notice what the oppressive caste system has done to the country and her majority people. It is obvious that they ignore the oppression and poverty of our people. Is economics the primary reason for this or is social injustice meted out by a degrading social system? Look at the conditions of most Dalits, whatever their religious affiliation. We should be ashamed for the part we have played in their deplorable condition.

We are faced with two Indias. During his presidency, President George W. Bush may have encouraged us all to revel in an "India Shining" in cooperation with our national marketing campaign, but what about the "India in Darkness" which is present in our streets, slums, towns, villages and forests — the India of the vast majority?

Upper caste India has to carry its historic shame and guilt and lead the struggle to abolish the caste system permanently in India. Upper caste India must develop a social conscience that intentionally includes the Dalits and the OBCs in all spheres of power: economics, education, politics, science and spirituality. This requires proportional representation. Upper caste India must embrace and entwine their lives, their future and their bloodline with Dalit-Bahujan India for the sake of their own children's future.

Despite the arguments, despite the controversies, and despite ever-increasing opposition, the most poignant aspect in the whole debate on conversion across the Indian nation is that there is simply no place in the Christian faith for forced, fraudulent conversions. Jesus never forced anyone to follow Him. God never forces, compels or deceives people into following Him. True discipleship involves a free will decision to follow Jesus and worship Him. Following the example of Jesus, Christians desire to meet the holistic needs of every person around the world so that everyone receives a positive life transformation and an abundance of blessings, with or without reservation or affirmative action benefits.

The motive and goal of Indian Christian love is not conversion, but instead to demonstrate the unconditional love of Jesus Christ to the untouchables of India. Christians believe we are commanded to love people and serve them whether there is thankfulness or not, whether the recipients follow Christ or not. This is the Christian community's firm stance on the topic of conversion, a stand we intend to maintain until the end. Those members of the anti-conversion conspiracy are simply using the term 'conversion' as the spark from which their fire of hatred and fear burns ever so fiercely. Dalits, however, in partnership with the Christian community, are ready to extinguish that flame.

In order for that flame to be put out, however, we must first confront the issue of caste in the most unexpected of places: the Christian Church.

CHAPTER EIGHT

CONFRONTING CASTE IN THE CHURCH

Bangalore, 2001: The dawn of the new millennium. Udit Raj's federation and the All India Christian Council (aicc) had organized the gathering and the hall was packed with an audience sitting in great anticipation of what was about to transpire. The traditional oil lamp was lit in front of a huge framed poster of Dr. B.R. Ambedkar, paying homage to a man who has yet to receive the full credit he deserves as one of the greatest socio-spiritual revolutionaries of the twentieth century.

Udit Raj spoke at length against the brutal oppression of the upper castes. He emphasized that without the affirmative action policies enshrined in the Indian Constitution, and without Ambedkar, he would have been sweeping gutters in his home state of Uttar Pradesh, North India. He explained that in the villages and towns of India nothing much had changed, even after 50 years of Indian Independence from British rule and a Constitution banning untouchability. He lamented that larger society continued its socio-spiritual caste prejudice and discrimination in defiance of the divine law of equality. He said that the way out was to eliminate the whole caste system, not to deal simply with its symptoms.

He announced that on November 4, 2001, he would lead hundreds of thousands of people out of Hinduism. "I was born a Hindu, but I will not die a Hindu," he declared, echoing Ambedkar's statement. A sense of outrage against the caste system filled the hall as he spoke.

It was then that I got up to speak. "We are here to express

full solidarity with the Dalits and the Backward Castes, and to bear their suffering and pain with them. I believe that now is the hour to draw a firm line against the caste system. We will stand with you and fight with you for your basic rights. Included in this commitment is the desire to empower you in every way we can. We have no ulterior motives. We simply want to demonstrate authentically the love of Christ to your people." I was happy to be able to make such a statement, sure that my colleagues around the nation would stand with me once they understood the full magnitude of the events unfolding before us in a great country like India.

As I finished my statement and sat down, I noticed that Mr. V.T. Rajshekar, a fierce spokesperson of the Dalit cause, rose from his seat. He came to the stage. He wanted to respond to my statement. My heart sank as I knew what was to come.

Unrelentingly, he attacked the caste system within the Church in India and asked if there was any initiative to do anything about it. He wondered why it had taken the Indian Christian community so long to take a public stand of solidarity with the Dalits and Backward Castes. He wondered whether the persecution by the Hindutva forces had anything to do with our seemingly fresh posture. He questioned the depth of our commitment to the Dalit-Bahujan people.

After his admonishment, however, he welcomed our support, recognizing that the global community must join together in the battle to deal with the evils perpetuated by the caste system. The Christian community could and should mobilize global opinion against caste discrimination. He expressed his concern that the upwardly mobile, English-educated elite working in the world of information technology and business was ill-suited to speak out on the injustices within Indian society. Who had the courage to speak against the practical slavery of the caste system in India?

Sitting on my chair on the stage, I realized there was no point in defending the sin the Indian Christian Church had been committing for centuries. One thing was crystal clear: Caste discrimination within the Church was a shame and stigma to the life and message of Jesus. It was a betrayal of Jesus' mission itself.

I stood up and I admitted that the Church in India was wrong and needed to repent. I admitted that the caste system was antithetic to Jesus' teachings about the Kingdom of God. I admitted that we had nothing to say in our defense and that we as the body of Indian believers should ask for the forgiveness of the Dalit-Bahujan people. I promised to seize every opportunity to demonstrate tangibly that we love the Dalit-Bahujan people and want to care for them. I explained that all human beings are made equal in the image of God, and that there is no such notion as the superior Brahmin and the inferior Dalit. I stressed the fact that Indian Christians must agree with Ambedkar's thesis in his "Annihilation of Caste."[1]

I am ashamed that the caste system has penetrated the Church in India, the caste system which surpasses white racial apartheid in its sheer evil against humanity. There is no real escape from the caste system; there is no upward mobility. Financial prosperity, though desired, does not remove the stigma of caste even when achieved. For caste-minded Hindus, Dalits do not deserve to prosper. Their lack of dignity is innate in their very existence. It is therefore the right of the upper caste to oppress the lower castes and Dalits. I have stated previously that the caste system and its attitudes make the Dalits the supreme victims of human civilization.

The fact that the caste system still survives and oppresses people is a dark blot on human civilization. Women, the Sudras (lowest caste), and the Dalits — the vast majority of people in India — are confined socially and theologically to the status of lesser human beings by virtue of birth. Their god is said to have created them unequal. Every sub-caste (over 6,000 in all) is placed in a divine hierarchy through birth. This caste system, codified by Manu over 3,000 years ago, surely surpasses everything else in the history of man's cruelty and oppression against fellow human beings.

At the human level, the roots of the caste system are in

the dark side of mankind: humans are utterly selfish, evil and without remorse. The dark side of man is capable of constructing and ordering religion and God in such a way that it justifies man's violence against his fellow man. It is capable of creating the collective conscience that legitimizes blatant injustice. Man's unwillingness to accept his true position in relation to his fellow man is the driving passion behind this and every other social evil.

At its root, social evil is sin against the Divine and His order. In this context, the pretext of religious traditions and practices is meaningless. Any saintliness, divine "enlightenment," or God-experience that is devoid of concurrent social justice and righteousness in all spheres of human life is the opposite of true religion. Sin against man is a sin against the Divine. By subscribing to the evils of caste, the Church in India is sinning against God.

Having learned and experienced the love of God, the Indian Church should know that the fundamental equality of all human beings is a self-evident truth. Equality is intrinsic to the makeup of mankind, however downtrodden and oppressed their current state. Modern genetic science has underscored the fact that we are children of the same stock and that underneath, the color of all our skin is identical and ultimately discolored by sin.

Tragically, the Indian Church has not yet learned this lesson fully. More than 50 years ago, the Christian Church failed Ambedkar and his people. We should have shown solidarity with that movement because those were difficult times. Today, unless there is tremendous reformation, the Church will again betray the Dalit-Bahujan peoples.

If the Indian Church engages in this huge socio-spiritual reformation happening within Indian society, its impact will be felt not only in India, but also around the world. This dynamic movement has the power to compel Christians everywhere to respond authentically to a world filled with pain, injustice and moral degradation. The Church must therefore respond in earnest to a world looking for authentic spirituality.

It is time for the Indian Church to act. The Indian Church needs to readdress discipleship with a hard look at the Indian social context. There are too many social inequities in the nation, too much social sin. The Christian faith inherently must challenge all sin. The present quality of Christian discipleship is too shallow to address the needs and challenges that the Dalit community brings to the Church. Christian discipleship in India as in other nations is "dualistic" and does not address the whole of life, thus our urgent need for developing holistic discipleship. Christian discipleship must deal with issues of personal, social and communal life. How can today's malformed Christian disciples bring the full dimensions of Christian discipleship to the Dalit masses?

The only way the Indian Church can move forward in their total acceptance of the Dalit-Bahujans and their total elimination of caste from the Church is to develop a local church-based model that meets Dalit-Bahujan needs. I believe that certain key elements should be at the heart and soul of the modern-day Church movement. This movement can then enthusiastically show the Church's genuine interest in breaking down all caste barriers.

First, top leadership in churches must include Dalits. This includes spiritual leadership, denominational leadership and lay leadership. Even today, many Church leaders cannot see that caste practice has divided and devastated the Church by segregating its leadership roles. Promoting the kind of unity Jesus wants requires abolishing the practice of caste discrimination on all levels in the Body of Christ. The Indian Church is more than 70% Dalit. The Scheduled Castes and Scheduled Tribes make up the larger part of the membership of all Indian Christian denominations, churches and organizations. If this is indeed true, then top leadership in the church must reflect this demographic. Leadership development programs should focus on empowering Dalit believers to exercise their spiritual gifts of leadership and pastoral care.

'Spiritual leadership' within the Church refers to the clergy. It is important to have Dalits in leadership positions like pastors, deacons, elders, bishops and overseers. Within the caste system, Dalits have been denied all spiritual rights including the right to the priesthood. Dalits desperately want the right to spiritual priesthood and the right to handle spiritual responsibilities of God. Dalits, like everyone else, have the spiritual commitment and capacity, but discrimination and bias in the Church prevents them from being empowered to hold higher leadership positions. Dalits in all levels of top leadership within the Church will be the beginning of bringing justice and righteousness to the Indian Church.

Second, conquering caste in the Church means allowing Dalit leaders in the Church to be involved in the financial management of the local Body. Too often in India, powerful upper caste leaders control the purse strings in all parts of society — including in the Church. Authentic Dalit emancipation cannot be realized unless there are qualified Dalits in significant management roles with regard to church finances. We believe the Church should stand out as the prime example of truly believing in the complete transformation and empowerment of the Dalits, most notably by empowering Dalits to handle top-level financial management.

Third, in its effort to bring true equality to its congregations, the Church should endorse inter-caste marriages. The final death of caste will be the mixing of the bloodline of Indians. This is what Dr. B.R. Ambedkar believed and enthusiastically proclaimed. Caste prejudice is seen best in the arranging and solemnizing of marriages. Church leaders can show their authentic attempt to rid the Church of caste by encouraging this possibility and personally demonstrating inter-caste marriage. Actions speak louder than words and Church leaders should be leading by action, especially in this regard. A highly respected Indian Christian leader commented years ago that in present-day India a Christian leader who had not affirmed and supported an inter-caste marriage through his own life, through the lives of his children, or through the life of some other blood relation was not fit to aspire to top Christian leadership in India. The "Majority India" of the Dalits and Backward Castes (as well as our friends among the upper castes) is looking for Christian leaders who live out gospel truths in the most intimate of ways.

Fourth, the religion offered to Dalits through the Church must be a religion that meets not only their spiritual needs, but also their felt physical needs. Religion has been used to both exploit and deal a cruel blow to the Dalits for 3,000 years. The Indian Church must not hide the real issues of human equality, dignity, opportunity, development, honor, hope and spirituality. The Gospel of the Kingdom must be of highest priority to the Indian Church and must be practically manifested in community and society. The Church's message to Dalit-Bahujans across the nation and around the world must eradicate the idea that Dalits are less than human, born-sinners, sinners in a past life, and born to be slaves to others. The Indian Church must give Dalits hope and resources to combat both the symptoms and the entire system that has oppressed them for so long. A Christian faith that is not authentic and true to the Gospel of the Kingdom as preached and taught by Jesus is not enough for the Dalits. The credibility of the Church and the value of the Dalit people require more. Much more.

The Dalits' fight must become the Church's fight.

Is the Indian Church ready to reexamine itself and step forward with actions that will produce church-based models as the answer for India's Dalit-Bahujans? Only time and a complete commitment by Indian Christians will eventually tell the story. For now, though, the Indian Church continues its steps of repentance in front of the Dalit people and moves forward with the hope that the principles of forgiveness and acceptance will be warmly embraced within the Dalit Freedom Movement and beyond.

This movement into the future will take energy, endurance, initiative, partnership and a clear agenda for hope and freedom. All of these put together will make a difference in the lives of individuals whose true-to-life stories will evidence a remarkable full-life transformation.

CHAPTER NINE

TRUE STORIES OF DALIT FREEDOM

The Dalit Freedom Movement is well underway and the Good Shepherd Church of India plays a vital part. We are standing against Brahmanism and offering partnership and hope. The emancipation of the Dalit-Bahujan people is no longer an impossibility; no longer an unreachable dream.

Validating these efforts are the personal stories of those whose lives have been transformed as a result of meeting Jesus, changing attitudes, a growing sense of equality, and global solidarity with the Dalit-Bahujan plight. The changes are remarkable and are both immediate and generational. The changes mark a positive future for more Dalit children and a generation of Dalit adults to bring an end to the bondage of caste domination.

Here are just a few stories from the lives of individuals whose lives have been eternally and holistically transformed

They fled their home, one step ahead of the law.

Kuni was too young to understand it, but in fact hers was a Dalit family living in poverty, with no education and few choices for employment, which had descended into criminal activity for survival. The sudden flight of her parents and siblings, along with the entire extended family, had been an escape before the adults were arrested, and children abandoned.

Their new home was no better than their previous

one: they were still relegated to a Dalit community where poor and marginalized families were crowded into impoverished neighborhoods. Improper sanitation, poor educational facilities for the children. It was one of those neighborhoods a higher caste person would not even enter for fear of being contaminated by the mere presence of Dalits.

Kuni grew up all too keenly aware that she was "untouchable." She knew she would face discrimination all her life. That's why she was so amazed when a team came to her village to show a free movie — and organized no special seating to keep the castes separated. She knew Dalits were never allowed to mix freely with other castes, so this new arrangement was very strange! Then, when the movie began, she became even more intrigued.

The film was *Dayasagar®*, an all-Indian acted Life of Christ motion picture. In English the title is *Oceans of Mercy*. The film introduces the story of the Lord Jesus with no cultural barriers to the gospel. It spoke immediately to Kuni, because she saw that Jesus loved everyone, from the high caste to those shunned from society. But then she also noticed that Jesus offered forgiveness of sins. This was something about which she had never heard. She wanted to hear more!

When the film ended, and the team offered people the opportunity to come to know Jesus as Savior, Kuni was excited to freely follow Christ. Further, she wanted her family to know Jesus, too. She began telling them about the living God, and about the film. She even arranged with the team to come and show the film for her family. Over the next few months, several of them also chose to follow Jesus. This was a tremendous turning point for the whole family, but there was more in store.

Our Good Shepherd Church movement focuses on holistic ministry. In Kuni's village, Dalits were living in unhealthy conditions, and there is little education about health and hygiene available to them. Our Good Shepherd Health Initiative team visited to do general health screenings and to teach Kuni's family and others in the village about healthier living.

Several members of the family were suffering from stomach parasites, and some of the adults, as young as men and women in their 30's, were suffering from undiagnosed diabetes. India has a high incidence of diabetes. Untreated, the disease can cause blindness, kidney failure, even death. But the Good Shepherd Health Initiative staff members were able to provide free medication to the neediest people. Today, Kuni's family is living healthier and is filled with more joy then ever before.

The arranged marriage is still well-accepted in India today. Poolama was an obedient young woman who married the man her parents had selected for her. Friends of the family recommended him. He seemed to be good "husband material." Poolama's parents loved her: they wanted to see her married so she would have a husband to take care of her. As Dalits, they were extremely poor and wouldn't be able to provide for their grown daughter forever.

At first, things went well. Poolama and her husband started their family, but some things began bothering Poolama. Her husband drank. They couldn't afford for him to spend money on liquor, so this became a major problem. Unless Poolama worked extra jobs, they couldn't feed their children. Then Poolama discovered her husband's infidelity. His addiction had led him into bad company. Soon he abandoned Poolama and the children completely.

This left the desperate mother of four in a terrible situation. An unmarried woman with children is at a huge disadvantage in India. If she's a Dalit with no education and no skills, it's even worse. She and the children could have starved. Thankfully her extended family took them in, but the home was cramped and overcrowded. And Poolama had to work 'til all hours at difficult, menial jobs just to keep food on the table. The future for her and her children looked bleak indeed.

Then she happened to meet a film team from the Good Shepherd Church of India. They were showing the *Dayasagar®* film in her village and invited Poolama to come and learn about the Lord Jesus. Poolama was enthralled by the story and soon chose to follow Jesus as her Savior. She even began telling her family and friends about Him and bringing them to see the film as well.

Her new faith brought new joy to her life, but she was still struggling for survival. This is why the Good Shepherd Economic Development program was so important to her. She began attending classes to learn about managing money and providing for her family. Just as importantly, she learned a trade, which the Economic Development program markets for her. Now she has valuable new skills and is earning a much-needed income. She and her children are all healthier because of the regular meals she can provide.

Today, because of God's grace extended through the Good Shepherd Church movement, there is happiness in their home and hope for the future.

✼

Four-year-old Raj had a job. A dangerous one. He worked in the firecracker factory. Although, "factory" was really too grand a word for the garage where Raj and other impoverished Dalit children and adults labored hour upon hour.

Sometimes Raj was emptying fireworks casings into a tin container in preparation for their being loaded, but most days he was one of the children stuffing explosive powder into the casings. There was the ever-present danger of a fire or explosion in the factory itself, but the worst side effect for Raj was that he was continually exhausted as his childhood slipped away. His family arose at 3 a.m. every morning to walk for three hours to the factory, then worked all day and walked home at night.

As Dalits, they had few options. But Raj's parents could see that this life was destroying their little boy. He remembers the day that instead of walking to the fireworks factory, they walked to a new place, a place that was strange to Raj: a Christian orphanage. With breaking hearts, his mother and father left him there with the hope that he would receive an education and perhaps have a better life than they could give him. Raj was devastated. He was too young to understand that his parents were trying to protect him. All he knew was that the family he loved had abandoned him.

The loneliness and bitterness might have been too much for the little boy if it weren't for *Dayasagar*®, the all-Indian acted Life of Christ motion picture. A Good Shepherd film team came to the orphanage to show the film. Raj was delighted with the character of Jesus on the screen, a wonderful Man who healed the sick, cared for the poor, and spoke with love and compassion. But when Jesus' enemies attacked and executed Him, Raj was stunned. *Why was this happening to such a good Man? Why did Jesus have to die?*

The film explained why: Jesus is the real God, the only true God, and He laid down His life because He loved Raj, and all people like him. The film's scenes of the resurrection and risen Savior touched Raj's heart. That day, he chose to freely follow Jesus personally. Now, when his teachers and friends at the orphanage talked about the Lord Jesus, Raj understood and was so happy to know that Jesus loved him and would never abandon him.

It was a kind of love Raj had never known! And it shaped his life. He went on to go to Bible school, then trained to become a film team worker, sharing *Dayasagar*® with others who needed to hear the Good News about Jesus. Later he accepted a position as a teacher at a Good Shepherd School. Today he is pouring into the lives of Dalit children the same joy and hope that was poured into his life at the orphanage.

It was like a wedding day. Except 17-year-old Kondamma was being wed to the goddess Yellama. After the ceremony at the temple, Kondamma was to become a *jogini*, or "ritual prostitute." The practice is centuries old: impoverished parents "sacrifice" a daughter by giving her to the temple as the bride of a goddess. Then the priests sexually abuse her and sell her to other men. Why would any parent allow this to happen to their daughter? There are several reasons ...

- They cannot afford to feed the child and will not be able to afford the dowry a prospective husband will demand to take her off their hands.
- They receive a monetary reward from the priests or temple in exchange for giving up their daughter.
- They believe they will receive the blessing and favor of the goddess in return for prostituting their child.
- They believe the goddess will bless their daughter so that when she is too old to be a prostitute anymore, and will return and care for them in their old age.

The dedication of young girls as temple prostitutes happens every day in India, especially among the Dalits, who are thought of as less than human anyway. And so it was with Kondamma on her "wedding day" at the temple. The ritual would unite her with the goddess, and then she would become a prostitute.

Not willing to allow this practice to continue, the Good Shepherd Church movement is dedicated to the prevention of human trafficking. Teams routinely endeavor to educate Dalits on the horrors of life as a jogini, the options parents have outside of this dreadful choice, and the fallacy of believing a jogini will one day return and take care of her aging parents: many die from AIDS, some from starvation and other diseases when they are too old to continue working.

Through Economic Development initiatives, the Good Shepherd Church movement promotes alternatives for Dalit and other poor families to provide for their daughters, and also educates

Dalits on human trafficking. And sometimes, when lives are at risk, the teams intervene directly. When they heard that Kondamma was about to be married to the goddess, they took the most direct action they could: they notified the police.

The ritual was immediately stopped! Kondamma escaped the horrifying prospect of enslavement as a temple prostitute! Now she and her family are learning about new and better ways to rise above poverty and discover their true worth and dignity in God's eyes.

Sometimes no one stops the "wedding" ceremony to the goddess. Even girls of 8, 10 or 12 years old are forced into temple prostitution. Valsama doesn't know whether her parents just wanted to get rid of her or if they believed they would be blessed with favor by the gods if they left her at the temple to become a jogini.

However it was that she came to be a temple prostitute, this was the nightmare of her life from the time she was a young girl: sexually servicing the priests and any man to whom they sold her.

At first men paid a high price to abuse and humiliate her. She was a great asset to the temple. But as she matured, she became worn-out and beaten-down. She bore two daughters (who were also destined to become jogini as the "property" of the temple). As she attracted less affluent clientele, Valsama knew the fate which awaited her, the same fate as generations of joginis who had gone before her. As soon as her daughters were old enough to be forced into prostitution, she herself would be sold away to a brothel where she would grow old and eventually be tossed out on the street to starve. There was also the horrifying possibility that she might contract AIDS and die.

But then something wonderful and unexpected happened: Valsama met a team of women from the Good Shepherd Anti-Human Trafficking Unit. They convinced her they could help her escape temple prostitution and start a new life! They would even support her with the funding to get her own spice press and spices to sell.

To Valsama, it sounded too good to be true — a way to escape the horrors of the life of a jogini and rescue her two daughters as well? Why would anyone help her in this amazing way? There had to be a catch. Surely the women wanted something from her, or would enslave her themselves if she went into debt to them. This is how Valsama first heard about the love of Jesus. The women on the team explained to her that the one true God loved her, and had called them to love her as well. They wanted to help her because all people are made in God's image and deserve freedom and dignity. Their offer came with no strings attached. It took courage for Valsama to trust this outlandish story, but she was desperate to protect her children if there was any possible way. She told the women she would accept their offer.

She was excited to see the spice-pounding machine and learn to use it. When she actually had her first bags of spices ready to sell, and held them in her hands, she was astonished. That day, when she made her first sale, tears of joy began pouring down her face. She was going to be able to provide for her children, not by selling her body, but by making and selling spice packs, honest work she could do herself. What an example she would be setting for her children! And what a relief to have escaped the bondage of human trafficking which is such a threat to Dalit women in India.

This encounter with the Good Shepherd Church movement transformed Valsama's life and future. She chose to become a Christ-follower. Her little girls will soon be enrolled in the English-medium Good Shepherd School, so their lives will be enriched as well. An English-language education will open tremendous doors for them moving forward. They will never have to fear being forced into ritual prostitution or starvation.

The story of this family's transformation is a beautiful example of the Good Shepherd Church's commitment to preventing human trafficking and helping the victims. Temple prostitution is a tradition of the majority faith in India, and flourishes among the poorest of the poor. But when joginis are given a practical way to leave the life and provide for themselves and their families, they experience hope and joy they never before imagined!

HIV-positive.

The test results were a death sentence.

As a young woman expecting her first baby, Krishna Veni was devastated. How could this be? The only man in her life was her husband Gopi. After they married, they had fallen deeply in love. She'd never been unfaithful to him. Lately he'd been moody, drinking too much, and terribly angry with her. His behavior had changed. He'd even begun beating her and taking the small salary she made working at a local school. She had to scrounge just to find food.

At first she'd hoped he would be excited about their first child. Maybe a new little life would change his terrible attitude and behavior toward her. But now ...

She told him about her diagnosis.

And he said he had known he was HIV-positive for a long time.

He just never told her.

He ordered her to abort the baby and continued to treat her with contempt. When she wouldn't have an abortion, he started beating her and kicking her belly in hopes of killing the baby inside.

Bruised, sick and hopeless, Krishna tried to kill herself. She threw herself down a well in hopes of drowning. If her father had not been coming to visit her, she would certainly have died. He rescued her and took her home with him. He was appalled at the way Gopi had treated his daughter, and heartbroken by her diagnosis.

But another shock awaited him at home: his wife, Krishna's own mother, refused to have her in the house! She was afraid of contracting HIV. Desperately, Krishna's father tried to find a place she could stay, but everywhere the neighbors refused to have her. Finally he left her in a derelict shack, promising to return as soon as he could. That's where Krishna's son Bunny was born. She delivered him herself, alone in an abandoned shack.

Somehow her husband found out where she was. He came and tried to strangle the baby! Krishna had to fight with him to keep the child alive. She was able to prevail because Gopi had by this time become weakened by the onset of AIDS. Three years later he died from the disease. Krishna herself carried his body to their home village and oversaw his cremation and the disposal of the ashes. Her in-laws, Gopi's family, seemed grateful to her for this and when her father offered to pay them to look after her and her son, they agreed. But two weeks later, they threw her out on the street. Her father was angry that things hadn't worked out. He refused to offer her any more help and once again, Krishna had nowhere to turn.

She took 3-year-old Bunny into the forest and expected they would starve there. But they were found by a woman who lived nearby and invited them to her home. Krishna began working as a housekeeper for her. For three years, she and Bunny had a home where they were happy. Her employer introduced them to a secular NGO working with people living with HIV/AIDS. Soon Krishna had gone through training to become a counselor and help other women in her position. She was starting self-help groups, working for women's rights, and more. Finally she was able to get life-extending medicine for her own condition.

But perhaps the best thing that happened, through her work she was introduced to a hostel for AIDS orphans, which would also accept Bunny. He could live there where he would have other children with whom he could play. Perhaps more importantly, though, he could attend a Good Shepherd School. Krishna was thrilled to know Bunny would be well cared for and get an English-medium education for his future. And all the while she could visit with him and remain an important part of his life, for as long as she should live.

Today Krishna has been diagnosed with cervical cancer. She is living at a Good Shepherd Health Initiative clinic, where she's receiving radiotherapy for the cancer, as well as her HIV treatments. Through Bunny's school, she heard the message of the Lord Jesus many times. It wasn't until she received the cancer diagnosis that she decided to personally follow Jesus. Come what may, she wants to know that there is everlasting hope for her and for Bunny. Although the future is uncertain, today there is joy for this little family as they move forward together, united in faith and in prayer for healing.

It is my hope that these encouraging stories of full-life transformation convince you that Dalit Freedom is possible. Let us work toward that end as a global community committed to the dignity of humankind. Let us eradicate caste from the face of the earth. Together we can transform lives and communities today and into eternity.

CHAPTER TEN

INTRODUCING FREEDOM

At the heart of the Good Shepherd Church movement is the belief that the transforming love of Jesus sets people free. The New Testament shows a model of church community that works perfectly in India, as believers disregard traditional caste restrictions, see every person as a valuable being made in the image of God, and band together to raise the poor and marginalized to a new way of living in Christ.

For this model to work, in its spiritual and compassionate aims, people must first experience the power of God's Kingdom message. Without Christ at the center, the program would lose its power. Our film ministry is one of the foundations of the movement: film teams carry the Life of Christ motion picture *Dayasagar*®, or *Oceans of Mercy,* across the nation. They show the film in large village presentations, in schools, hospitals, private homes — wherever people are able to come and see the movie.

The film features Indian actors and Indian settings. It has been dubbed into the major languages of India. It speaks in a dramatic way both to the illiterate and to those who can read, both the well-to-do and to the utterly impoverished.

Among the Dalits, it is a revelation, an amazing discovery that there is a God who made them in His image and loves them as His own children. It shows that this God is the one true God, that He endows them with dignity and worth just by virtue of His love for them. This is astonishing Good News for those who have been taught they are worthless, sub-human and cursed by the gods.

Meeting Jesus is a transformative moment for a Dalit. It can change the trajectory of their lives — and set them free! And there is so much more ...

1. Thousands of Good Shepherd Churches, which in turn become centers for the spiritual development in the village.
2. Good Shepherd Schools, providing more than 30,000 Dalit and other poor children with a critically important English language education. This can be a key to a young Dalit's advancement into higher education and a career.
3. Job Training Centers that help Dalit adults develop practical skills which can move them out of poverty.
4. Economic Development programs — currently thousands of Good Shepherd Self Help Groups in Dalit communities are learning to band together and improve their lives with grants for small business.
5. Good Shepherd Healthcare Workers and Clinics. These workers and clinics are strategically placed in the neediest areas to help with medical assessments and treatments, health and hygiene education and much more.

Each of these programs is critically important for Dalit freedom.

The Good Shepherd strategy works to engage villagers with Jesus, establish a church as the foundation for improving their lives, and elevate the entire village to a new way of living.

The Good Shepherd Community Church movement helps propel Dalits and other poor and marginalized people to a brighter future in a village-based, church-based holistic way. The eternal hope of Jesus Christ brings great joy and the practical, compassionate aid and education provided make a tremendous difference in the here and now.

India's Dalits have been enslaved to caste-based discrimination for far too long. It is a privilege to be able to introduce them to the freedom of new life in Christ. We welcome your partnership in sharing God's hope with people in India in great need. Thank you.

END NOTES

Introduction:
[1] See The Foreign Exchange of Hate: IDRF and the American Funding of Hindutva, 2002, by Sabrang Communications & Publishing Pvt. Ltd, Mumbai, India; and The South Asia Citizens Web, France. http://stopfundinghate.org/sacw/ index.html. In addition, see "In Bad Faith?" by AWAAZ, 200, http://www.awaazsaw. org/ibf/.

Chapter One:
[1] See The Hindu, October 19, 2002, "Cow's life very important: VHP," by Neena Vyas.

[2] See "Village Terror," Frontline Magazine, Vol. 24, Issue 6, March 24-April 6, 2007, by T.K. Rajalakshmi.

[3] Human Rights Watch, Broken People, Bangalore and New York, 1999, p. 41.

[4] i.e., The Scheduled Castes and Scheduled Tribes [Prevention of Atrocities] Act, 1989, and rules in 1995. Also Article 338 of the Constitution was amended several times to set up the National Commission for Scheduled Castes.

[5] Article 17 abolishes "Untouchability." Its practice in any form is an offense punishable under law. No article in the Constitution was adopted with such unanimity and so great an acclamation and enthusiasm as this article. To enforce this law, in 1955 "The Untouchability Offenses Act" came into force. The 1955 Act was

amended in 1976 and came to be known as "The Protection of Civil Rights Act." One significant new provision of the Act is that a person convicted of an untouchability offense will be disqualified from running for public office.

[6] Under article 330, 114 seats are reserved in the Parliament and 691 seats are reserved in the state assemblies.

[7] National Crimes Bureau Report, Crime in India 2006, Chapter 7, "Crime Against Persons Belonging to SCs / STs," http://ncrb.nic.in/cii2006/home.htm.

[8] Untouchability in Rural India, by Shah, Ghanshyam and Harsh Mander, Sukhadeo Thorat, Satish Deshpande and Amita Baviskar, New Delhi: Sage Publications, 2006.

[9] Dalit oppression, a dark reality, by Aasim Khan, CNN-IBN, Nov. 12, 2006, http://www.ibnlive.com/news/dalit-oppression-a-dark-reality/26025-3.html.

[10] Freedom's just another word, by Harsh Mander, Hindustan Times, Aug. 15, 2006 — see http://www.hindustantimes.com/StoryPage/StoryPage.aspx?id=94c60a18-edef-4d6f-b156-4a8d51b171a6.

[11] Frontline Magazine, "Untouchability unlimited," by S. Viswanathan, March 15, 2008; http://www.frontlineonnet.com/fl2506/stories/20080328250603900.htm or http://indianchristians.in/news/content/view/1639/48/.

[12] For a vivid description and compelling stories on the challenges for Dalits in Tamil Nadu, please see Dalits in Dravidian Land, by S. Viswanathan, New Delhi: Navayana Publishing, 2005.

[13] Dalits are denied right to food: Study, By Vineeta Pandey, Daily News and Analysis, Nov. 3, 2007, http://www.dnaindia.com/report. asp?newsid=1131338&pageid=0.

[14] "Dalits remain unempowered," The Asian Age, May 30, 2008; http://www.asianage.com/presentation/leftnavigation/news/india/ dalits-remain-unempowered-.aspx or http://indianchristians.in/news/ content/view/2123/48/.

[15] "A crap job," by David Griffiths, New Statesman, May 28, 2008, http://www.newstatesman.com/2008/05/india-caste-manual-dry-work. For more stories and information about manual scavenging in the state of Andhra Pradesh but also the challenges across India, please read India Stinking, by Gita Ramaswamy, New Delhi: Navayana Publishing, 2005.

[16] "Dalit women invisible citizens: Report," The Hindu, June 24, 2008; http://www.hindu.com/2008/06/24/stories/2008062459960600. htm.

[17] "Dalit girl crosses the hurdle," Times of India, by Arabinda Mishra, Aug. 20, 2005; http://timesofindia.indiatimes.com/ articleshow/1205566.cms; and "Mamata Nayak can now cycle to college," The Hindu, Aug. 30, 2005; http://www.hindu. com/2005/08/30/stories/2005083002232000.htm.

[18] UN Committee on the Elimination of Discrimination Against Women, 37th session, Concluding Observations: India, 2007; http://www.unhchr.ch/tbs/doc.nsf/(Symbol)/CEDAW.C.IND. CO.3.En?Opendocument.

[19] "Manual scavenging still rampant in North East Delhi, says report," by Parul Sharma, The Hindu, May 18, 2008; http://www.hindu. com/2008/05/18/stories/2008051853440400.htm.

[20] "Manual scavenging: Time to clean up our act," by South Asia Human Rights Documentation Center, Oct. 31, 2005; http://www.hrdc.net/sahrdc/hrfeatures/HRF129.htm.

[21] "Hidden Apartheid," by Human Rights Watch, 2007; http://www.chrgj.org/docs/IndiaCERDShadowReport.pdf.

[22] p. 43, 45; U.S. State Department 2006 Country Reports on Human Rights Practices, March 2007, http://www.state.gov/g/drl/rls/hrrpt/2006/78871.htm.

[23] "Broken People: Caste Violence Against India's Untouchables," March 1999, by Human Rights Watch; http://www.hrw.org/reports/1999/india/.

[24] http://chrgj.org/docs/Narula%20May%202007%20Testimony.pdf.

[25] See "Not Quite Like Us," by S. Anand, Tehelka Magazine, Vol. 4, Issue 45, Nov. 24, 2007; http://www.tehelka.com/story_main36.asp?filename=cr241107not_quite.asp.

Chapter Two:

[1] The tribal people are called Adivasis, which means "the original inhabitants." The Hindu fundamentalist forces did not like this term because it implied that all others were intruders or invaders. Therefore, they preferred the term "Vanavasis" or "jungle people" because most of them lived in the jungles and were chased by the invading Aryans who seized the land of the original inhabitants.

[2] Priests (Brahmins), rulers or warrior kings (Kshatriyas), the common people (Vaishyas), and servants (Sudras). Their creation from the mouth and other parts of the primordial man is described in Rig Veda 10.90. For details of The Law of Manu please refer: Wendy

Doniger O'Flaherty and Brian K. Smith, The Law of Manu, Penguin Books, New Delhi, 1991.

[3] Manu prescribed that they should live near mounds, trees, cremation grounds, in mountains and in groves, recognizable and making a living by their own innate activities. They should live outside the village, and dogs and donkeys should be their wealth. Their clothing should be the clothes of the dead, and their food should be in broken dishes; their ornaments should be made of black iron, and they should wander constantly.

[4] Personal email correspondence from John Dayal, October 18, 2004.

[5] According to James Massey, "Historically, the roots of the term Dalit go back even to the pre-Biblical Hebrew and pre-classical Sanskrit era. Its ancient form is found in the east Semitic group of languages, especially known as Akkadian. The present usage of the term Dalit goes back to the nineteenth century, when a Marathi social reformer and revolutionary, Mahatma Jotirao Phule, used it to describe the outcastes and untouchables as the oppressed and broken victims of our caste-ridden society." Massey 1994, 6.

[6] The term 'Dalit' could also use any of the following definitions: the torn, the rent, the burst, the split, the opened, the expanded, the bisected, the driven asunder, the dispelled, the scattered, the downtrodden, the crushed, the destroyed, the manifested or the displayed.

[7] For comprehensive statistics on daily discrimination faced by Dalits, see Untouchability in Rural India, by Ghanshyam Shah, Harsh Mander, Sukhadeo Thorat, Satish Deshpande and Amita Baviskar; Sage Publications: New Delhi, 2006.

[8] UN International Labor Office, Report of the Director-General, 2005, p. 31.

[9] Of Inhuman Bondage, By Steve King, p. 94.

[10] "Missing, a strong legal framework to combat child labor," by Azera Rahman, Indo-Asian News Service, June 11, 2008; http://www.indiaenews.com/india/20080611/124262.htm.

[11] p. 8, Social Dimensions of Child Labor: Dalit Children in Hazardous Industries, by Aradhana Yadav, New Delhi: Indian Social Institute, 2007.

[12] Child Labor Prohibition and Regulation Act, 1986, No. 61, and Child Labor Prohibition and Regulation Rules, 1988.

[13] p. 52, Social Dimensions of Child Labor.

[14] p. 79, Social Dimensions of Child Labor.

[15] "Trafficking of SC, Dalit girls," Times of India, Feb. 20, 2006.

[16] Vitasta, 2006.

[17] Tom Brake MP, excerpt from transcript of debate in Hansard, England, on the topic of slavery. See www.parliament.the-stationery-office.co.uk.

[18] Mr. Asbjørn Eide and Mr. Yozo Yokota (E/CN.4/ Sub.2/2003/24), June 26, 2003.

Chapter Three:
[1] Constitution [Scheduled Castes] Order, 1950; http://lawmin.nic.in/

ld/subord/rule3a.htm.

[2] See Chapter Seven.

Chapter Four:
[1] In 1927, as a protest, Ambedkar burned the law book Manusmriti which was against traditional caste restrictions.

[2] http://www.state.gov/g/drl/rls/irf/2006/71440.htm.

Chapter Five:
[1] "Periyar, the propagandist," by M.S.S. Pandian, The New Sunday Express, Sept. 17, 2006, p. 27.

[2] ibid.

[3] ibid.

[4] http://en.wikipedia.org/wiki/E._V._Ramasami_Naicker.

[5] A full feature-length film was released in 2007 in India about Periyar's life. See "Periyar was against Brahmanism, not Brahmins," April 30, 2007; http://www.rediff.com/news/2007/apr/30inter.htm.

[6] The Week, Nov. 18, 2001, p. 17-18.

[7] If unseeables come out during the day, they are said to pollute others just by being visible. Thus, such people are only allowed to come out of their home after sunset and go back home before sunrise.

[8] Dalits were expected to maintain a graded distance from the different levels of upper caste people: 33 feet from the lower group;

66 feet from the Brahmins (quoted by Devasahayam 4).

Chapter Six:
[1] See website http://www.expressindia.com/latest-news/Question-mark-on-motive-Was-anticonversion-law-really-needed/334642/.

[2] See "The Confusion Called Conversion" by E. Sunder Raj, ELS: Madras, 1991.

[3] For further analysis, see Acts of Bad Faith: Report on Anti-conversion Laws in India, South Asia Human Rights Documentation Centre, January 16, 2007; http://www.hrdc.net/sahrdc/hrfeatures/HRF157.htm.

[4] From Beyond Caste: SC upholds OBC quotas in central educational institutes, April 11, 2008, Times of India.

[5] Note: Supreme Court ruling on April 10, 2008, upheld reservation of 27% for Other Backward Castes in higher education, and for reservations for teachers of high-ed institutions. "Ashoka Kumar Thakur vs. Union of India and Others" was writ petition (civil) 265 of 2006. This decision upheld a law passed by Parliament in 2006, called the Central Educational Institutions [Reservation in Admission] Act, 2006" and was immediately challenged on May 22 by anti-reservation proponents.

SELECTED REFERENCES

Chandra, Ramesh (ed.), Dalits and the Ideology of Revolt, New Delhi: Common Wealth Publisher, 2003.

Chandra, Ramesh (ed.), Dalit Identity in the New Millennium, Vol. 1-10, New Delhi: Commonwealth Publishers, 2003.

Chandra, Ramesh (ed.), Dalits and their Future, New Delhi: Common Wealth, 2003.

Chandra, Ramesh, Phases of Dalit Revolt, New Delhi: Commonwealth Publishers, 2003.

Chaudhary, S.N., Dalit and Tribal Leadership in Panchayats, New Delhi: Concept Publishing Company, 2004.

D., Manohar Chandra Prasad, Broken God Broken People: The Plight of Dalit Christians, Bangalore: Rachana Publications, 1996.

Das, K.C, Indian Dalits, Delhi: Global Vision Publishing House, 2004.

Devasahayam, V., Doing Dalit Theology in Biblical Key, Madras: Gurukul, 1997.

Devasahayam, V., Frontiers of Dalit Theology, Madras: Gurukul, 1997.

Deulkar, Sita, Dalits Past, Present and Future, New Delhi: Dominant Publishers, 2004.

Doniger, Wendy and Brian K. Smith, The Laws of Manu, New Delhi: Penguin, 1991.

Dalitology: The Book of the Dalit People, Tumkur: Ambedkar Resource Center, 2003.

Dr. Babasaheb Ambedkar Writing and Speeches, Vol. 1-8, Bombay: Education Department of Government of Maharashtra, 1982.

Fernandes, Walter, The Emerging Dalit Identity: The Re-Assertion of the Subalterns, New Delhi: Indian Social Institute, 1996.

Franco, Fernando; Macwan, Jyotsna; and Ramanathan, Suguna, Journeys to Freedom, Samya, 2004.

Ghosh, G.K., Dalit Women, New Delhi: A.P.H. Publishing Corporation, 1997.

Human Rights Watch, Broken People, New York: Books for Change, 1999.

Irudayaraj, Xavier (ed.), Emerging Dalit Theology, Madras: JEST: TTS, 1990.

Kumar, Vijendra, Rise of Dalit Power in India, Jaipur: ABD Publisher.

Lal, A.K., Dalit in Action, New Delhi: Concept Publication, 1997.

Madan, G.R, Casteism Corruption And Social Development in India, New Delhi: Radha Publication, 2004.

Mathew P. D., Constitution of India, New Delhi: Indian Social Institute, 1996.

Michael, S.M. (ed.), Dalits in Modern India: Vision and Values, New Delhi: Vistaar Publication, 1999.

Mohanty, R.P., Dalits Development and Change, New Delhi: Discover Publishing House, 2003.

Nirmal, P. Arvind, A Reader in Dalit Theology, Madras: Gurukul Lutheran Theological College and Research Institute, n.d.

Nirmal, P. Arvind, Towards A Common Dalit Ideology, Madras: Gurukul Lutheran Theological College and Research Institute, n.d.

Omvedt, Gail, Dalit Visions, Orient Longman, 2006 (reprint).

Paswan, Sanjay (ed.), Encyclopaedia of Dalits in India, Vol. 1-11, Delhi: Kalpaz Publication, 2002.

Prabhakar, M. E. (ed.), Towards A Dalit Theology, Delhi: ISPCK, 1989.

Prakash, Surendra, Concise Manu Smrti, Delhi: CIRSR, 2000.

Prasad, Ravi, D. M, Dalit Youth: A Sociological Study, New Delhi: APH Publishing Corporations, 1997.

Puri, Harish. K., Dalits in Regional Context, Jaipur: Rawat Publication, 2004.

Pylee, M. V., An Introduction To The Constitution of India, New Delhi: Vikas, 1995.

Samuel, Swapna H., Dalit Movement in South India, (1857-1950), New Delhi: Serial Publications, 2004.

Shah, Ghanshyam (ed.), Dalits and the State, New Delhi: Concept Publishing, 2002.

Shah, Ghanshyam; Mander, Harsh; Thorat, Sukhadeo; Deshpande, Satish; and Baviskar, Amita, Untouchability in Rural India, New Delhi: Sage Publications, 2006.

Singh, Buta, The Dalits and Dalit Awakening in India, New Delhi; Gyan Publishing House, 2004.

Singh, Mahender, Dalits in India, New Delhi: Reference Press, 2003.

Sivaprakasam, M.V., Dalits and Social Mobilization, New Delhi: Rajat Publications, 2002.

Teltumbde, Anand, Anti-Imperialism and Annihilation of Castes, Ramai Prakashan, 2005.

Tripathy, Rebati Ballav, Dalits: A Sub-Human Society, New Delhi: Ashish Publishing House, 1994.

Verma, D.K. (ed.), Ambedkar Vision and Education of Weaker Sections, New Delhi: Manak Publisher, 2004.

Viswanathan, S., Dalits in Dravidian Land, New Delhi: Navayana Publishing, 2005.

Zelliot, Eleanor, From Untouchables to Dalit: Essays on the Ambedkar Movement, New Delhi: Manohar Publisher, 2001.